when the lights go down

The story of cinemas of a Midlands town

MAURICE THORNTON

Published by

MELROSE BOOKS

An Imprint of Melrose Press Limited
St Thomas Place, Ely
Cambridgeshire
CB7 4GG, UK
www.melrosebooks.co.uk

FIRST EDITION

Copyright © Maurice Thornton 2014

The Author asserts his moral right to
be identified as the author of this work

Cover designed by Tanya Fukes

ISBN 978-1-909757-01-1

Printed and bound in Great Britain by:
Grosvenor Group (Print Services) Ltd
London

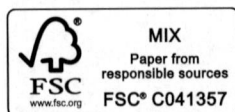

MIX
Paper from
responsible sources
FSC
www.fsc.org   FSC® C041357

CREDITS

I acknowledge the following contributors and establishments who have helped in the production of this book, without which it would have not been possible.

DAVID ALLEN – DOUGLAS ASHBY – COLIN BALL – M. BALL – COLIN BAMFORD – DAVID BRADSHAW – ALAH BUKSH – P. CHRISTIE (Scunthorpe) – P. COWAN – MRS P. COWAN – J. COPLEY – CARMEL CRAWLEY – JANENE COX – SU DAVIES – MAVID DODSON – ADRIAN DUFFEY – GEORGE DUNKLEY – IRENE FALLER – REG. GOODMAN- MRS. GOODMAN – TOM HAYCOCK – S.M. IRONS – BRIAN McFARLANE – MARGARET McMANUS – C.T. MARLOW – GEOFF. MARLOW – SHIELA MILLIGAN – B.G. OLD – DAVID PRYKE – MALCOM ROBINSON – BRADLEY SALMON – LEWIS J. STANLEY – CHARLES W. THURSTON – BERYL TINY – EDDIE TOSELAND – W. WAKEFIELD (Rtd) – MISS P. WATSON – RICHARD VOWLES – STANLEY WHITE – S.J. WINFIELD – MARION WILLIAMS.

THE BRITISH FILM INSTITUTE
BOROUGH OF KETTERING
BRIAN HORNSEY – Ninety Years of Cinema in Kettering
KCBC FM RADIO
KETTERING BOROUGH COUNCIL
KETTERING PUBLIC LIBRARY
KETTERING REFERENCE LIBRARY
KETTERING MUSEUM

NORTHAMPTONSHIRE NEWSPAPERS LTD. - EVENING TELEGRAPH
RANK LEISURE LTD – ODEON THEATRES
CHARLES WICKSTEED LTD.
The person who kindly sent me, anonymously, the Savoy opening souvenir programme. The programme has now been placed in the Kettering Museum for archival retention.

2014

The Regal, Kettering - December 1936
(Photo: J. Winfield)

CONTENTS

Preface   ix

Part 1: Introduction: 1
         when the lights go down

Part 2: The Bioscopes: 5
         Walk up, Walk up. See the Pictures that Live

Part 3: The Cinemas of Kettering   10
         The Corn Exchange   10
         Vint's Electric Palace/The Palace   13
         Hippodrome   16
         Victoria Hall/Victoria Picture House   20
         The Victoria Picture House   25
         The Odeon   30
         The Avenue Theatre   37
         The Coliseum – New Coliseum   39
         Savoy   48
         The Studios – Ohio Cinemas   58
         Kettering Electric Pavilion – Gaumont Pavilion   65
         Gaumont   72
         Empire – New Empire   77
         Regal   86
         Granada   98
         Odeon 8-Screen Multiplex   105

Part 4: The Other Picture Shows   111
         K.I.C.S. Central Hall   111
         Working Men's Club, Wellington Street   115
         Miniature Rifle Club & Rifle Band Club   118
         Town Band Club – Windmill Club   121
         The Wicksteed Park   122

Part 5: Yarns, Customs and Personalities   124
         Silent Cinema   124
         Personalities   134
Part 6: The Years of War   140

Part 7: On Stage and Screen   145

Part 8: The Little Gems   151
         1. Electric Palace/Bentley's/Ohio – Burton Latimer   151
         2. Electric Picture House/Ritz – Desborough   159
         3. The Picture House/New Picture House – Rothwell   168

Part 9: Cinema Clocks   181
         ODEON – Kettering   181
         Regal – Kettering   182
         Empire – Kettering   182
         Savoy – Kettering   183
         Gaumont Electric Pavilion – Kettering   183
         Working Men's Club Cinema – Kettering   183
         Electric Palace Burton – Latimer   183
         Picture House – Rothwell   184

Part 10: The Final Reel   185

Chronological History   187
Glosary   191
About the Author   195

PREFACE

The cinemas of Kettering hold a special place in my life. Like so many of my generation, they were a part of my childhood, growing up into adult life, and so to the present day. Going to the pictures is still an occasion, and remained so throughout my career as a projectionist. To have worked in a Kettering cinema, especially as it was a boyhood favourite, was a pleasure no other period in my working life has ever matched.

In my first book I was able to make a record of the existence of Kettering cinemas of the past, setting down their stories and their contribution to the life of the town, which might otherwise have been lost forever. They each had a fascinating tale to tell of how they emerged and the people that built them. Each had a character and style of their own, adding much to the period of time that they existed.

There are few reminders of past cinema heritage today. Most of the buildings have long since gone or been given over to other uses. Future generations will have little knowledge of where the Savoy, Regal, Electric Pavilion, Empire, or Odeon once stood. Good reason then to have written the first edition of this book and to write a new edition.

The book has been compiled from material first researched to December 1997, with further research to 2012. With little written about some other cinemas that existed within around a dozen miles of Kettering, short descriptions of picture houses of Thrapston are included, as well as a section about Watts cinemas in Finedon and Irthlingborough.

Every attempt has been made to achieve accuracy and it must be appreciated that, with a work of this depth, some omissions and errors may occur. Photographs and illustrations have been hard to come by and some are not of the quality wished for, but they are the only ones available, so my apologies and I hope they do not detract from the enjoyment of the book.

Students of cinema and media subjects, who are undertaking research on, or reading about cinemas featured, or indeed any cinema subject, are welcome to seek information from the Author.

Maurice Thornton

Part 1

INTRODUCTION
when the lights go down

The murky London fog swirled around a dimly-lit Leicester Square on a March night in 1896. Across the square from the old Alhambra, its rival – the bold, brash Empire Music Hall – was advertising the miracle of the age. The theatre was brightly lit by its four large standard globe lights, whilst three more beneath the canopy illuminated the large sign over the entrance doors advertising the '*Cinematographe Lumieres*'.

Within the lively interior, the full house eagerly awaited the start of the experience of their lives. They had heard of the revelations of just two weeks before when Felician Trewry had presented the *Lumiere Cinematographe* show to a paying audience in the nearby Regent Street Polytechnic for the very first time. Now the Empire audience waited with great expectation to witness this new phenomena called 'living pictures'.

The house lights dimmed to just the little gas lamps, and the audience was hushed in the near darkness, as a beam of light from the back of the hall threw a large picture of people outside of a factory onto a large screen stretched across the stage. In this picture the people moved back and forth, and as the images changed constantly, the audience sat open-mouthed with disbelief at what they were seeing. Their eyes were perceiving but their minds were unable to take it all in. As the film ran through the cinematograph, and the scenes changed to a train coming into a station, some were so disturbed they hurried from the hall. It was as if magic powers had been unleashed upon them.

That public showing of the Auguste and Louis Lumiere films

1

on their Cinematographe, is considered to be the birth of cinema in Great Britain. The show ran for fourteen months at the Empire and the programmes were changed regularly, showing films made also by British cinematographers, including Birt Acres and Robert W. Paul.

Robert Paul was by this time exhibiting films on his Theatrograph at the Alhambra opposite, and Leicester Square began its associations with cinema which lasts until today. A reporter, writing in a popular magazine of the day, stated that *Cinema had arrived and was an immediate hit. To see carriages roll up outside the Empire would suppose that Leicester Square had only just been discovered.*

By the end of that year, the Cinematograph had spread to over seventy cities and towns in the country, and Bioscope shows were finding their way into halls and music halls, thrilling those who attended. The showmen of the day were quick to see the potential of this new and exciting entertainment, and they converted side-shows into Bioscopes virtually overnight. Some of these showmen moved ultimately into converted and purpose-built halls as, by 1909, cinema was going indoors. The 1909 Cinematograph Act was legislated to regulate the new industry and put an end to the safety problems being encountered. The showmen also saw the all year-round business opportunities, and by 1914 the Bioscopes had left the fairgrounds and gone indoors.

Kettering's cinema history starts with the showmen, for it was on the fairground that the 'living pictures' – or 'animated pictures', as they were generally known – made their debut. It is with certainty that the first Bioscope show to a paying audience took place on the Recreation Ground during Feast Week of 1897. The first Bioscope show to a paying audience in a hall seems to be the one advertised as being given by Mr. Warren East at the Victoria Hall in 1901. There may have been other shows, perhaps at the Corn Exchange, but there is no evidence found. The Corn Exchange was showing animated pictures as part of the variety bills from about 1903. The Victoria Hall and the Avenue Theatre also booked stage shows which included a Bioscope presentation, or a touring show which included one.

Cinema in its own right started in 1909 with Vint's Electric Palace, which was a conversion of the Corn Exchange. It remained the major venue for motion pictures until the first purpose-built cinema arrived in the form of the Kettering Electric Pavilion in 1913. In 1920 the Victoria Hall was converted into a cinema, and in that year the Empire – a new purpose-built cinema – opened in Eskdail Street.

Meanwhile, the Avenue Theatre had become the Coliseum and then the New Coliseum. The Victoria Picture House – the former Victoria Hall, Kettering's elite cinema – was to see another conversion in 1936, when it became the much-loved Odeon. It was the town's first super-cinema, but not for long. At Christmas that year, the super-duper Regal opened its doors and it was reckoned to be one of the best cinemas in the county.

The last cinema to be built was the phoenix-like Savoy, which rose from the ashes of the ill-fated New Coliseum, and opened in May 1938. We must not exclude the 'sixth' cinema in the town, at the Working Men's Club, who began regular weekend and holiday time cinema in their concert hall in the early 1930s.

Around Kettering there were other cinemas which provided entertainment for their communities, and they all feature in this edition. The Electric Palace at Burton Latimer, The Electric Picture Palace/Ritz at Desborough, Plaza at Thrapston, and, of course, the Watts cinemas at Burton Latimer, Finedon and Irthlingborough.

One by one these little cinemas have gone. The Odeon 8-screen multiplex continues the cinema tradition. In their heyday, the five Kettering cinemas provided over 5000 seats between them; one for every regular picture-goer in the town at that time. You would be lucky if you got one of them on a Saturday night after 7pm.

This story of the cinemas is not a requiem to their passing, but a celebration of their existence and of the wonderful medium that was their reason to exist. It is about the entrepreneurs, and those who worked in the cinemas and loved them. It is about enterprise and the social history of communities.

For those who can remember them and loved them, I hope memories will be re-kindled. For others too young to have experienced the cinema of yesteryear, this book provides an interesting background to your present day movie experience in your multiplex. Movies have been around for a long time, and the old cinemas of Kettering are a part of that heritage.

When the lights go down the screen illuminates with living pictures in temples created for them. The CINEMA

Savoy, Kettering stage presentations for the last week of November 1939
(Photo: M. Thornton)

Part 2

THE BIOSCOPES
Walk up, Walk up. See the Pictures that Live.

As you walked into the fairground on the Kettering Recreation Ground in July of 1897, the bustle that accompanied the Victorian fair engulfed you. The atmosphere was electrifying. The air was filled with that smoky aroma that distinguishes the steam engine from any other. The electric lights were dazzling and of a magnitude not repeated between the annual Feasts. In the centre of the ground stood the mighty showmen's engines, noiselessly generating the power for the fair, their immaculate liveries matching the beauty of their mechanical excellence.

Around and about, the fair was in full swing. The *Four Abreast Galloping Horses and Ostriches* was fully loaded with punters, screaming with delight. Other large rides filled the centre of the fairground, whilst around the sides were the countless sideshows that travelled with the fair, each providing the 'sensations of the age', from the *Siamese Twins and the Two-headed Snake* to the *Horrors of the Wax Museum,* boxing booths, and other attractions.

The show that stood out from all others in this year of 1897 was the new Bioscope, proclaiming the latest sensation of 'living pictures'. Before its centre steps, the crowd watched with amusement the troupe of dancers as they danced to the music from the mechanical organ. The Barker was enticing the crowd to 'walk up and witness the greatest magical show ever – living pictures. See the boxing kangaroo. See the acrobat on a pole and the boxing dogs'.

Parting with two pence at the box office entitled you to crush into the tented area, with rows of benches right down to the small stage, on which a large white screen was erected. At the rear was a strange-looking machine, smoke escaping from its chimney; a lens and a bright light could be seen inside. In the dim light, the machine whirred as the operator turned the handle and magical moving images were thrown onto the screen.

The audience responded to every movement and trick on the screen, and at once the moving pictures had captured the minds of the Kettering Feast crowds, and cinema had come to town.

Showman William Taylor had converted his mechanical sideshow into a Bioscope in 1897. This show had toured, presenting dioramas, but with the coming of the cinematograph – like other showmen of his time – Taylor saw the potential pulling power of the new invention, and he began the 1897season with his Bioscope show. He was to bring the show to Kettering for nearly twenty annual Feasts.

Charles Thurston, Senior, although a riding master, brought the fair to Kettering; and the family still do to this day. He was also an important developer of the Bioscope. He built the *Original Royal Show* and brought it to Kettering in 1901. This Bioscope show was a grand walk-up sideshow, with a two-wagon front. In 1909, however, it was rebuilt to an organ front. The interior was standard tented, with wooden forms as seats. The show had its own attendant engine, which was usually the Burrell No. 2462 'Queen Alexandra' and later Burrell 2780 'King Edward VII'. Friendly rivalry between the two showmen saw them trying to outdo each other, which was all the more exciting as they would often be side-by-side on the fairground.

In 1907, Taylor brought a larger Bioscope show to the Feast. The marquee was said to hold hundreds of people, and with it, he brought his new larger fair organ – a 104 key Marenghi.

Thurston's Great Show. An organ fronted 'walk up' Bioscope featuring a 120 key Marenghi organ (Photo: Fairground Society)

Not to be overshadowed, Charles Thurston presented what some people of the day said was his greatest achievement, *The Great Show*. It was a combination of Bioscope and Vaudeville, and was large in every way. A walk-up show, built by Orton and Spooner, the ornate carved panels and moulded uprights were said to be worth walking many miles to see.

It had a giant fair organ, a Marenghi 120 key, built by the famous Paris organ builder. The organ, like the Bioscope show, was illuminated by hundreds of electric lamps, which changed colours to the beat of the music (what price the disco outfits of today?). The organ outplayed everything else on the fairground and could be clearly heard above the general din of the fair. The interior of the Bioscope sported velvet seating, and its tapestry-hung walls were a luxury not seen on any fairground elsewhere. It was managed by John. H. Norman and was perhaps the first 'super' cinema.

On the stage front of the *Great Show,* comics and dancers would perform their crowd-drawing acts. Inside the marquee was a large stage and screen, where the variety acts were performed and the 'living pictures' were shown. Admission was 3d. The films shown were repeats, with some local interest included. The attendant engines are recorded as being 2462 Queen Alexandra and the newer 3075 Alexandra.

Records show that in 1907 a device called the 'Chronomegaphone' was included in a Bioscope show. This device, with a linking synchronism between a gramophone and the projector, provided a sound accompaniment to the pictures. It is not clear whether it was the Taylor or Thurston show, as both seem at some time to have presented these first attempts at 'talkies'. While the device was quite successful, it was less than satisfactory because the sound output was no greater than that emitted from the gramophone horn, so people further back could not hear it.

The bioscope shows attended the Kettering Feast weeks until 1914, and around that time they were taken off the road. The reasons were three-fold. Although Taylor and Thurston were very responsible showmen, others were not, and up and down the country serious mishaps befell Bioscopes, both on fairgrounds and in buildings, particularly with fires. So legislation had been brought in to deal with this.

Secondly, popularity – especially for travelling Bioscopes – was beginning to wane and cinema was going indoors. Both Taylor and Thurston were pioneers in this field, and met the challenge by building cinemas. Taylor built the cinema at Calne. Thurston built the **Empire** at Biggleswade, the **Cinema Palace** at Norwich – both long gone – and the **Electric Palace** at Harwich, which still operates today.

Thus cinema moved indoors from the hustle and bustle of the fairground and established itself as the premier entertainment of the age. The showmanship of William Taylor and Charles Thurston brought the Cinematograph to Kettering and, although their visits were only once each year, they brought the very best of moving pictures available at that time.

Between the years of 1901 and 1909, many travelling Bioscopes visited the town showing complete film programmes or as part of stage presentations. There were also local cinematograph operators; one notable person being Warren East, who by 1907 had assembled a complete company, providing music, dialogue, song and the cinematograph.

Travelling Bioscope shows toured the country and were booked as part of variety shows or as complete performances, such as the W.C. Poole Myrioama, The Walturdaw Bioscope Company and the St. Lawrence Picture Company, all presenting complete 'living picture' shows.

The first recorded 'indoor' bioscope show found so far was performed in the Oddfellows Hall, Desborough in 1897 (destined in future years to become a cinema), six months after Taylor's arrival on the Kettering fairground. Such was the success of cinematograph in Kettering that in 1909 the town was to get its first permanent cinema.

Part 3

THE CINEMAS OF KETTERING

The Corn Exchange

One of the prominent buildings of mid-19th Century Kettering stands on the Market Square. It has seen many uses and alterations in its time, and for a while it was the first cinema in the town.

In 1853 the town was in need of a 'market exchange' and meeting rooms. Kettering was a thriving town and there was also the need for a town hall. Francis Edmund Law of Northampton was required to draw up the designs for a Corn Exchange on the Market Place, and in due course the building was erected at the cost of £2,950.

It contained a market room on the ground floor and an upper room, which served as the town hall. The upper room was to the front of the building, over the entrance and offices. The market room took over the remainder of the building and had a semi-circular roof, part of which was glazed and supported by cast iron pillars. The building was of brick, and the front elevation was stone-faced with central wooden doors. The Corn Exchange opened in 1854. At some stage, a public library was housed there.

The main usage was such that during the day it served as the Corn Exchange when required to do so. At other times and in the evenings it was used for meetings, lectures, concerts, balls and exhibitions. It was also used for lantern shows and, later, cinematograph shows.

Such a performance was held for the week of 10th February, 1903, and was a particularly interesting one, as shown in this reproduction.

The Corn Exchange – Kettering
Monday February 10th. 1903 for six evenings

Jasper Redfern presents

THE ELECTRIC DISOLVING STEREOSCOPE
FEATURING

ANIMATED PICTURES & ANGLO AMERICAN VAUDEVILLE
Animated subjects include
• **THE DELHI DURBAR CELEBRATIONS** •
• **THE DENABY COLLIERY EVICTIONS** •
• **A TRIP TO THE MOON** •
• **ALI BABA AND THE FORTY THIEVES** •

plus **20 STAR ARTISTES 20**

SEATS 2/- 1/6d 1/- 6d.

Doors open at 7.30pm (Early doors at 7pm 3d. extra)

A typical travelling Bioscope Show programme 1903
(Photo: M. Thornton)

The programme was a touring show and the cinematograph was set up at the rear of the hall. The report in the *Evening Telegraph* the following evening seems to suggest that it was a re-opening after closure, for the installation of electricity in the Exchange:

The Corn Exchange was well-filled last night when Mr. Jasper Redfern's Company gave another splendid entertainment and patrons had the opportunity of seeing the Hall alighted with electricity which with its use also saw the illuminating display of his electric dissolving stereoscopic pictures. The photography was supreme and in natural colours. Vaudeville entertainment was exceptionally good with Mr. Herbert Betts being a most culpable comedian and Mr. W. E. Eel being a cleverly accomplished ventriloquist. The singing of Miss Ada Gray and Mr. Lucien Gray was of charming description. There should be crowded houses throughout the week right up until Saturday night.

From this report, it seems that Jasper Redfern had entertained at the hall before, possibly bringing a cinematograph using a different light source, but it is interesting how it is described as an 'Electric Dissolving Stereoscope'. A cinematograph was certainly used to have shown that programme. In all probability more animated picture shows featured at the Corn Exchange, but by 1909 the building was redundant. A new Corn Exchange had been built in London Road and the new Public Library had opened in Sheep Street.

The time had come for Kettering to have a permanent home for the burgeoning business of cinema, and begin the excitement and glamour so craved for by its patrons.

The Corn Market Hall before conversion (Photo: unknown)

Vint's Electric Palace
The Palace

Leo Vint, of Long Acre, London – already an owner of cinemas – purchased the old Corn Exchange building and gave Kettering its first permanent cinema. He converted the interior and used part of the upper room to construct a balcony. The projection room was built at the rear of the balcony and constructed out of sheet iron. The seating in the balcony and rear stalls was red plush.

Vint presented stage turns and pictures twice nightly, at 7pm and 9pm, and advertised the acts as being supported by first class pictures. Prices of admission were Stalls 2d. 3d. and 6d. Seats in the balcony were 9d. The general manager of the theatre was Mr. Arthur Brogden. Vint's Electric Palace opened on the evening of 16th October, 1909 with a programme of variety and pictures, presenting American song vocalist Miss St. Malo and Mr. Harry Coombes, and first class pictures on the screen.

Kettering's first cinema
(Photo: unknown, probably local press)

A following newspaper report had this to say:

The immediate success which attended the opening of Vint's Electric Palace was probably unprecedented in the annuls of local entertainment. This new Palace, as most people are aware, is installed in the one-time Corn Exchange and the proprietor and manager have set out with the fixed idea of giving the public what it wants and have been immediately rewarded by the crowded response to the two performances. The site upon the Market Place was a very unusual one. Brilliantly illuminated the front of the Palace gave a good appearance to the place. A large crowd was waiting for admittance to the second house before the first had been released and two constables had to be placed before the doors to keep order.

Inside both the splendid furnishings and excellent programme more than fulfilled the promises made. The old corn Exchange is quite unrecognisable in its new arrayment every corner of the building being used to its best advantage. The programme was a very long one displaying pictures of the most up-to-date kind with songs and dialogue to the films.

On the façade, the four main buttresses of the building were etched with the words: COMEDY, DRAMA, TRAVEL, and OPERA. During this period, proclamations were often read from the theatre steps. Possibly a retainer from the days when it housed the town hall, a photograph of the time shows the proclamation of King George V being made there. Interesting to note that to the right of the entrance were the Covington's Geisha Tea Rooms. There did not seem to be the usual billboards associated with a cinema anywhere on the exterior walls at that time.

Leo Vint continued ownership of the theatre until 1912 when Mr. John Covington, a Kettering tradesman, leased the property and changed the name to the **Palace**. A private company was formed, known as the Palace (Kettering) Ltd. and registered on the 14th June, 1912 with a capital of £5000 in £1 shares. There were two partners besides Covington, namely Mr. G. Foster and Mr. G. Johnson. The pictures were advertised as being shown on the Palacescope, but is not recorded whether this was a projector or some publicity gimmick.

During the next two years the Palace was very successful, with many famous stars of the stage appearing on its boards. Included were Harry Tate, Lilly Langtry, G.H. Elliott, and many others. Pictures were also popular and one typical programme of Covington's early period was that of week commencing 18th December, 1912. The 'Bouncing Dillons', an acrobatic act, shared the bill with 'A Peep Behind the Scenes' (Edison 1912).

Though no actual dates are recorded, it seems that an attempt at 'talking pictures' was made by placing actors behind the screen to read the captions supposedly spoken by the silenced players in the films. One such drama was 'The Bells of Doom' (1912).

By the middle of June 1914, the theatre was in the hands of the Official Receiver, and Covington purchased the rights. He made further alterations and reopened in the August, running it with his two partners until they left for the Great War.

Covington changed the name to The Palace in 1912
(Photo: unknown)

Hippodrome

At the beginning of November 1917, the Palace had changed hands once again; this time to Mr. Fred Hawkins, of Peterborough. The reasons for the change are obscure, though it might have been that Covington was in financial difficulties. The theatre opened on Saturday, November 3rd with a new name, The **Hippodrome.** Hawkins made a number of changes in addition to the name, by dropping stage acts and making performance of films continuous.

The opening programme, however, did include variety acts – a practice which became traditional on cinema opening nights – with a rather strange item under the name of 'Pops Concert Party'. Afterwards it seems that variety did cease at the Hippodrome and it became a cinema, in direct competition with other cinemas opening in the town. Children's shows were run on Saturdays at 2.30pm.

Style of programmes remained almost the same for the next three years until Christmas 1920. After the week of 27th December, the cinema probably did not open, as the last shows advertised for that week were Monday to Wednesday 'Johnny, Get Your Gun' and supporting was 'All At Sea'. From Thursday to Saturday, showing was 'Thirty A Week', 'Pipe Dreams', Topical Budget (a newsreel), Episode 4 of a serial, 'Black Secret' starring Pearl White, and the heavyweight championship matches between Becket and Moran, plus Lewis and Basham.

There were no further advertisements following that week, and it is presumed either the Hippodrome closed or continued without publicity. The partnership between Covington, Johnson and Foster was dissolved in June 1922, and Covington is reported to have continued the operation until January 1923 when the Hippodrome closed with a formal notice by the Official Receiver. After a lengthy receivership case in the courts, a report in the *Kettering Leader* of 9th February, 1923 spoke of Covington having debts of £12,921 as and being a cinema owner and manager. No mention is made of Hawkins.

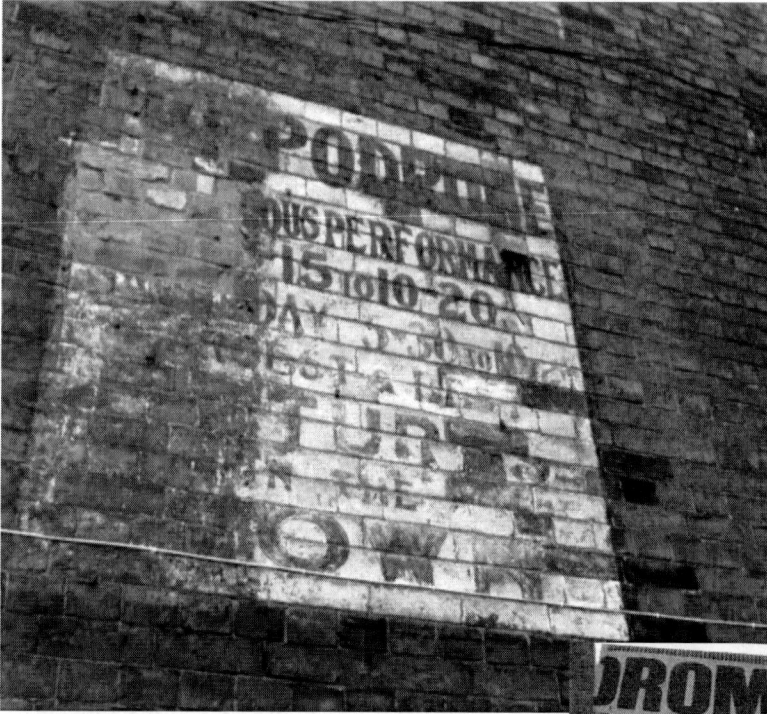

*This advertisement was painted on the side wall
of the cinema in 1917 when it was renamed
Hippodrome. It is still visible today after
restoration. (Photos: M Thornton)*

After further legal proceedings, the judgement
was made as expected and was concluded by
the statement that the whole affair had been
abysmally dragged out and the business
lamentable. The dates between the last
advertised programme and the Receivership
arc lacking in reported detail, and it can either
be assumed that programmes did continue at
the cinema or it was actually closed.

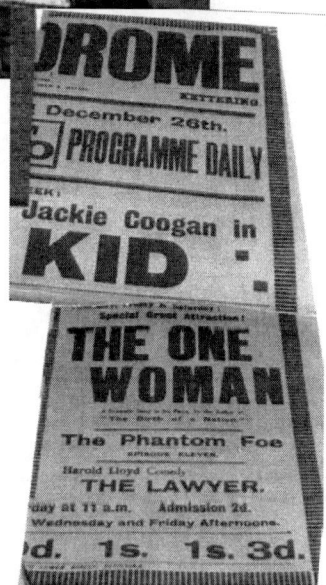

*Hippodrome publicity.
Date unknown.*

Mr. Fred Hawkins announces the opening of the

KETTERING HIPPODROME
(Late VINGTS PALACE)

Monday November 3ᴿᴰ. 1917
Continuous programme 6pm to 10.45pm

VARIETY AND PICTURES

POPS CONCERT PARTY
variety

- - - - - - - - - - - - - -

PICTURES
• SECRETS OF THE SUBMARINE Serial part 1 •
•PEARL OF THE ARMY •
Pathe serial part 1 starring PEARL WHITE
News from the Front Line

SEATS 2d. 3d. 4d. 6d. Balcony 1/-

Opening programme of the Hippodrome 1917
(Photo: M. Thornton)

Today the building remains. Reminders of earlier times can still be found on its walls. The words on the buttresses remain and, after restoration, the advertisement for the Hippodrome still remains, pronouncing 'continuous performances' and 'the largest and best pictures in town'.

Projection and technical information

Corn Exchange:

No projection permanently installed. Film programmes were provided by touring Bioscopes, etc. Projectors not known, but likely makes such as Wrench and Powers.

Vints Electric Palace

One Gaumont Chrono projector, front shutter. By the date of installation, was fitted up with top and lower spool boxes using a slide lantern as a light source. Later, two such projectors may have been installed, probably Powers.

Palace

Two projectors may have been in situ and likely those already installed. Gaumont Chronos or Powers are also likely. Reference to a 'Palacescope' is interesting, as no such make of projector has been found. Could have been a publicity gimmick.

Hippodrome

No detail found but, with five reeler features, certainly two projectors were installed and – at a guess – Powers No. 6, Ernemann, or possibly Gaumont Chronos. Carbon arc would have been the light source.

Sometime in the years 1910 to 1918, a Chronomegaphone was installed, but research fails to determine by whom or when. It is probable that Arthur Brogden and Fred Hawkins would have used the system. It is known that 'pictures with sound' took place in those years using a Vivaphone system developed by Cecil Hepworth, cinema pioneer.

The property still exists in commercial use – 1997. (Photo: M Thornton)

19

Victoria Hall
Victoria Picture House

It has become a part of Kettering. A vein of life-blood in the town. So it was said of the Victoria Picture house, when it closed its doors to be modelled into a modern cinema. By that time, the building had served the town for forty-eight years as a place of entertainment, much of it of an excellence. It held a special place in the hearts of theatre-goers and cinema fans alike.

The Victoria Hall was built to fulfil a need in the town. Apart from the Corn Exchange, public amusement was limited to the two Gaffs in the town; one being a portable theatre erected for travelling shows, which became a permanent theatre in Field Street, and later a second one run by Mr. Wild, situated in Newland Street. There was no large public hall in the town. The Corn Exchange had only limited seating and the newly-formed Kettering Public Hall Company took the opportunity to remedy the need.

Kettering was undergoing rapid changes at this time and reconstruction was taking place in Gold Street. Cottages, houses and small shops had been pulled down below the site of the Fuller Chapel, and a range of new shops was built by the Kettering Post Office Buildings Company. The centrepiece of this development was the Kettering Post Office and Arcade. To the west of this new property stood a three-storey mansion which had been the home of Mr. Fredrick Wallis, one of the founders of the clothing factory, Wallis and Linnell. Mr. Wallis died in 1887 and the property came onto the market. Seeing opportunity to continue the development of Gold Street, the Kettering Public Hall Company purchased the site. They swept away the old house, and construction of a new public hall was commenced by builders Margett and Neal, to the design and plans by Gotch and Saunders. The hall was to be named the **Victoria Hall** in recognition of the Jubilee of Queen Victoria, which was being celebrated at that time.

The new hall was built with a long foyer, the main body of the building being set well back from Gold Street. The street frontage was of two arches, the right one – on facing the building – was the public entrance to the auditorium, and the other a shop owned firstly by Horn and Robinson, who were piano dealers, then later by the Northamptonshire Printing and Publishing Company, and finally by Thos. H. Day, stationers which included the Victoria Circulating Library. Offices were accommodated on the first floor.

The official opening date is unclear, as it could have been Sunday, December 18th, 1888, but there are conflicting newspaper reports that it was either 1887 or 1889. Considering the time needed to construct such a large building, 1888 seems the most feasible.

Regardless of the doubt about the date, there is no doubt about the success of the grand opening performance

The Victoria Hall, Gold Street. 1889–1920.
(Photo: unknown)

of Handel's *Messiah,* followed by a rousing sermon by the then famous atheist orator, Charles Bradlaugh. The hall was filled to capacity to hear the Kettering Choral Society enchant those present with spirited and accurate renderings of the famous oratorio, to the accompaniment of an orchestra of local musicians.

The large stage accommodated the Society comfortably, and the ample orchestra pit filled with musicians. Never before had a Kettering audience seen and heard anything like it. The excellent acoustical properties were complimentary to the designers. One wonders at the boldness of the proprietors to follow the great religious work with an oration by Mr. Bradlaugh, and can only speculate as to how the audience reacted.

To the front of the street entrance were two ornate gas-lamps, their globes displaying the words 'Victoria Hall'. The entrance foyer was long and narrow leading to the auditorium. There was also a stairway leading to the balcony and gallery. Two corridors ran parallel to the auditorium, which led patrons to the body of the hall. The seating in the hall was removable and, combining the fixed seating in the balcony and gallery, could hold between 1000 and 1200 people. The interior was tastefully decorated and accommodation very comfortable.

The stage was fifty feet wide and thirty feet deep, equipped with full stage lighting of the day and four trap doors. There were four dressing rooms backstage and an ante-room, which could be used as a kitchen.

The hall was used for a multitude of purposes. There were, in addition to stage presentations, public meetings, bazaars, balls, concerts, and from time to time 'animated pictures'. The building also saw use as a drill hall. Charles Saunders, of Gotch and Saunders, used the hall for Mission services which later moved to the Tordoff School.

Alf Bailey, noted for his Kettering music business, provided musical accompaniment with his accorded String Orchestra. He was later to become an important figure with the hall. It would appear that from 1900 the Victoria Hall was presenting stage productions almost constantly, and typical of these would be performances of some of the great melodramas of the day. One such presentation was the play 'Star of Hope', staged by the Miss Wynn Miller Company and presented by the Victoria Theatre Company.

The use of the cinematograph in the hall is not recorded until March 1901, but visiting shows were bringing the new medium regularly as part of their programme.

As far as can be determined, the first advertised cinematograph show in the Victoria Hall was for the two evenings of March 12th and 13th; Mr. Warren East, a well-known local businessman and lanternist, was responsible for the presentation and operation of the show. A reproduction of the advert featured in the *Evening Telegraph* is shown.

THE VICTORIA HALL
KETTERING
TUESDAY AND WEDNESDAY MARCH 12TH. & 13TH. 1901

WARREN EAST'S

**LIVING PICTURES
ENTERTAINMENT**

WAR · COMIC · GENERAL SUBJECTS

SONGS BY MR. W.EAGLE · PIANO MR. ALF BAILEY

PICTURES INCLUDE

SCENES AND EVENTS IN THE LIFE OF H.M. QUEEN VICTORIA
THE COMPLETE FUNERAL OF OUR BELOVED QUEEN
TOUR OF THE OPHIR · ENGLISH CUP FINAL
SCENES OF A SOLDIERS LIFE IN AFRICA

BALCONY 1/6   FRONT SEATS & GALLERY 1/-
BACK SEATS 6D

A Warren East 'Living Pictures' presentation
(Photo: M. Thornton)

The show was well-received, as this report of the 13th March shows:

Mr. Warren East, the well-known lantern exhibitor, provided a capital cinematograph entertainment for the public in the Victoria Hall which was well filled by a delighted audience. A number of views were first thrown on the screen depicting the splendid manner in which the soldiers have to contend with things in time of (the Boer) War. These were then followed by short films of a number of comic subjects. During a short interval songs were contributed by Mr. W. Eagle and were loudly applauded. Mr. Arthur Turner also merited the recognition of the audience by giving a few selections from the phonograph

Proceeding with the cinematograph entertainment a number of comic pictures were thrown on the screen after which an excellent description was given of the late Queen Victoria's funeral thus enabling those who were deprived of the opportunity of witnessing that historical event to be able to form some idea of the proceedings. A peculiar effect in the final scene is obtained by the hundreds of visitors in Hyde Park gradually raising their umbrellas in the falling rain which appears then like a giant mushroom forest. Concluding the pictures were views of the mausoleum where the beloved Queen was laid to rest.

The programme also included films, 'Opening Parliament', 'Tour of the Ophir', 'English Cup Final', and some local films.

Thus the pattern of entertainment at the Victoria Hall was being set for a number of years to come, with the insertion of 'film sets' as regular features in shows, in between plays and even meetings. One notable instance in the use of the cinematograph was with the appearance of 'Poole's Myrioama Combine', which included Doctor Monnitschews Wonder Animal Acts. This was billed for the week of February 2nd, 1902.

Poole's was a famous travelling show which presented a whole programme of entertainment, usually of historic and topical tableau with music and spoken word. Judging by the newspaper report reproduced below, Poole had visited Kettering previously, although not with the Cinematograph. Poole would save the pictures until the last part of the show when, with musical accompaniment and oratory, he would show scenes and events far removed from the staged tableau for which he was accustomed.

One of the best variety entertainments which is placed before the public of Kettering is brought at regular intervals to the town by Mr. W.C.Poole. On Monday his company commenced a week's visit to the Victoria Hall. To say that the large audience was delighted would be but a mild way of expressing their appreciation of the rich treat provided. For fully three hours the interest was maintained and indeed the programme was so immensely varied that to say anyone had experience a dull moment would be grossly liable.

Mr. Poole's endeavour to make the entertainment attractive was by bringing his splendid pictures up-to-date and his collection of this occasion contained illustrations of the more sterling events in the recent South-African War. Many other striking national events are introduced and there is also a fine series of historical tableaux presenting the Battle of Waterloo. The Myoriama is a most agreeably diversified variety of entertainment.

In 1907, Alf Bailey – involved as Bailey and Company theatrical entrepreneurs – took over the Victoria Hall, and it became a theatre. Many famous artistes and theatrical companies were to tread its boards, and frequent visits by London companies ensured that Kettering audiences were treated to great shows of the era, such as 'Our Miss Gibbs', 'The Merry Widow', and the 'Arcadians'.

Pictures were now very much a part of the presentations, and touring Biograph shows appeared frequently. In 1908 the theatre was advertising the 'Walturdaw Bioscope Company presenting a programme of films', which included the Pathe part-coloured 'Cinderella', an epic of over 1000 feet in length made in the Pathecolour stencil process; a classic of its day.

The Victoria Hall was to spawn many notable local musicians, and the theatre orchestra gave regular concerts. The Sunday celebrity concerts were staged right up to 1920, featuring famous artistes and military bands.

The Victoria Hall closed the week of 5th April, 1920. The final show was by Basil Mitchell's London Company presenting the play, 'The Lowland Wolf'. The Victoria Hall changed hands with a ceremony on stage on the Saturday night. The hall was to undergo a massive alteration and become a cinema. Work on the conversion started immediately under the direction of the newly-formed Victoria Company. Shareholding was increased, and a number of local dignitaries were elected to the board. There appears to be no further record of Alf Bailey's involvement.

The Victoria Picture House

Conversion of the Victoria Hall involved removing the gallery and completely constructing a balcony, with raked seating giving clear views of the stage and screen. The seats were upholstered in crocodile leather and of the tip-up type. Behind the new balcony, the Victoria Tearooms were built, though did not open until some time later.

The projection room was constructed behind the stage, thus giving rear projection. The screen was translucent and its surface khaki in colour. It was 'flown' for the purpose of stage presentations. The existing windows in the hall were removed and replaced by new decorative

The Post Office buildings in Gold Street early 1920s
(Photo: D. Wharton)

panels, giving an elegance to the hall. The exterior was also changed. The two arches were demolished and replaced by a wider entrance and foyer. Over the new entrance, a canopy was erected in cast-iron and glass, complimenting the Post Office Buildings façade. This major reconstruction lasted eighteen weeks.

The new cinema opened on Monday, August 23rd, 1920, with 'Ragamuffin' (1916), starring Mary Pickford. Supporting were 'Wild Waves and Women', 'Ideal Varieties', and a Pathe News. The opening night was a great success and welcomes were given by the General Manager, Arthur E. Melbourne, and the Board. The programme continued for the first half of a split week, and on the Thursday the programme changed to 'The Common Cause' (1918), starring Herbert Rawlinson, 'Who's With Baby', 'He's A Devil', and a Pathe News.

THE VICTORIA PICTURE HOUSE,
GOLD STREET, KETTERING.

General Manager ... ... ARTHUR E. MELBORNE.

MONDAY, TUESDAY & WEDNESDAY, August 23rd, 24th and 25th,
MARY PICKFORD in

:: THE RAGAMUFFIN. ::

A World's Favourite Artiste in a Picture which stands alone.

Wild Waves & Women, a Sunshine Comedy. Ideal Varieties. Pathe Gazette.

THURSDAY, FRIDAY & SATURDAY, August 26th, 27th and 28th,
One of the Greatest Pictures of the Year:

THE COMMON CAUSE,

A Vitagraph Drama of Intense Interest. "I don't like it, so don't do it."
Who's With the Baby, Comedy. He's a Devil. Pathe Gazette.

MATINEE FRIDAY at 2·30. EVENINGS: Doors open 6 o'clock Continuous Performances 6.15 to 10.35

Admission: 6d., 9d., 1/-. Balcony 1/6. Reserved 2/-. Tax included.

— ORCHESTRA. —

Tip-up Seats throughout by Bobby, Ltd., Bournemouth. LUNCHEON, TEA and SUPPER ROOMS will be opened as soon as Alterations are completed.

Programme for the opening week in
August 1920 (Photo: M. Thornton)

Extracts from a rather long press report indicate that impressions of the new cinema were eagerly reporting that all the windows had gone, and in their place were tall panels gracefully decorated with shades of green and framed in white. Other panels of a similar design were tinged with a delicate buff. Each panel was surmounted by a white fibrous plaster, which included a decoration, and shaded wall lamps mounted on a pink relief. Electroliers suspended overhead provided the main illumination. The balcony viewed from the floor of the house apparently gave a particularly pleasing impression, with circular mounted plasterwork picked out in white. The report continues.

After being shown to your seat by the neatly-attired usherettes in rose-coloured dresses, one notices the absence of the overhead 'milky-way' by which the pictures travel to the screen. Explained, it appears that the projectors are behind the screen thus the picture being brighter and clearer and the auditorium avoids the dense Egyptian darkness as is usually associated with picture shows. Mr. White, the operator, as well as all male members of the staff, were ex-serviceman. Mrs. Melbourne, the musical director, was at the keyboard of the upright grand piano supplied by Alf Bailey.

The Victoria Picture House did not abandon stage productions, however. The original stage had been preserved in the alterations, and for many years the Kettering Operatic Society presented shows there. There were other stage presentations, but it was first and foremost a cinema. In the beginning Mrs. Melbourne provided the accompaniment on the upright grand piano, but shortly after the opening of the cinema she was leading a quartet. And in 1926 there was a sextet led by Maurice Friedman, who became an accomplished local musician in his own right. By 1928 the cinema had a full orchestra of ten musicians, led by another well-known musician, John Sugden. So good was this orchestra that it played musical interludes during intermissions and between films.

During the life of the 'Vic', as it was popularly known, it saw the advent of the 'talkies'. Contrary to expectations, the Vic was the first to show 'the talkies'. The first sound film shown, according to advertisements, was in the programme for the week of 9th June, 1929, when the short 'Cavalier Rusticana' was shown, featuring the Celeste Octet. That was followed by a film dramatisation by Bransby Williams from Charles Dickens' 'Bleak House', which was titled 'The Characterisation of Grandfather Smallwood'. From Wednesday, July 1st to 3rd, 'The Raw Recruit' was screened, with Ernest Latinga and featuring his well-known stage scene, and the following week George Robey was to be seen in a talkie short, 'The Barrister'.

These screenings are substantiated by the reviews in the *Evening Telegraph*, which said:

The talkie showing this week at the Victoria Picture House features Ernest Latinga in his hilarious sketch 'Raw Recruit' which seems to rectify the chief fault Kettering audiences have found in the talkies which is lack of action.

It would appear that the Vic was showing 'talkies' as early as June 1929, six months before its competitor, the Electric Pavilion. As there are no other reports of 'talkie' presentations before the 9th of June, the Victoria Picture House must stand as being the first in the town to show 'talkies'.

Gradually, sound films found their way on to the screen, though many programmes were still generally silent and some of the greatest silent films played at the Vic. It was styled as the best picture palace in town and it certainly was, with its plush furnishings

The Picture House
(Photo: D. Wharton)

28

and atmosphere of class. It is said that its balcony was one of the finest examples around and matched anything to be found in Leicester or Northampton, and all of this for just 6d., 9d., and 1shilling in the stalls, and 1/6d. and 2shillings (reserved) in the balcony.

The Victoria Picture House was to continue its business into the 1930s, presenting talkies to ever-increasing audiences.I can only dimly remember the very long foyer with its display windows. I do remember, however, the poster displayed outside advertising the film for the week of closure, and that was 'Come Out of the Pantry' (1935), with Jack Buchanan and Fay Wray.

The Victoria Picture House closed with the last performance on Saturday, April 24th, 1936. It was not without some sadness and, although a new modern cinema was to take its place, this report from the *Kettering Leader* at the time perhaps best sums up the local feelings:

> *Losing an old friend*
> *On Saturday night the owners of the Victoria Picture House closed their doors on a past of entertainment and social activity as one of the oldest public halls in the town. The Vic, dear to the hearts of many because of its many memories they have for it has had a long career. It has become a part of Kettering, a vein of life-blood of the town and it is not without a sigh or regret that it now closes its doors as the 'Vic' forever.*

Projection and Technical Information

Victoria Hall

The Victoria Hall had no projection equipment, as such. Cinematograph projectors were supplied by the travelling Bioscope shows or visiting presenters, such as the instance of Warren Eagle. Invariably, the cinematographs could have been virtually any of those made at the time, such as Wrens, Gaumont Chronos, or similar. The screen was presumably a roll-up type, or may have even been painted on the back wall of the stage. Following the Cinematograph Act 1909, there must have been a projection room of sorts, though there is no evidence of this.

Victoria Picture House

Rear projection was built behind the stage wall. The screen, likely 'flown', was translucent, thus letting the projected image 'through' and enabling sight from the auditorium. It was khaki in colour. Projection was via prisms. Projectors installed were two mute Kalee 7s modified. The sound installation was British Talking Pictures. The sound until around 1931 was sound-on-disk, the installation was Vitaphone. Speakers were installed by the proscenium arch. There is a possibility that when optical recorded sound became available (1928), a dual sound system using the Photophone system may have also been installed. It is likely that the Kalee 7s were changed to Kalee 11 Specials, which were dual sound system machines. The first three acclaimed talkie features, 'Jazz Singer', 'Lights of New York', or 'the Singing Fool', do not appear to have been shown at the Vic.

The Odeon

Every Saturday morning where do we go
Getting up to mischief? Oh dear, no!
To the Mickey Mouse Club
With our badges on,
Every Saturday morning at the ODEON.

Of all the cinemas in the town that offered Saturday children's matinees, perhaps the Odeon is best remembered. I cannot recall whether it was the first, but it was certainly regarded as the best. At least, that is what the kids of my generation thought; after all, it was showing lots of Mickey Mouse and Flash Gordon serials. The club chant, recalled above, was reverently sung and shouted every Saturday morning to a level that could be heard in Gold Street; such was the fervour of over 700 kids in the cinema.

The Odeon was constructed from the shell of the closed Victoria Picture House. On January 16th, 1936, the new Odeon (Kettering) Ltd. Company took over the old Picture House and closed it after the last show on April 24th.

Odeon (Kettering) Ltd. was a subsidiary of Odeon Theatres Ltd, headed by cinema entrepreneur, Birmingham-based Oscar Deutsch. By that time,

The Odeon Gold Street
(Photo: T. Smith)

his empire was expanding rapidly with over 200 cinemas nationwide. The sum involved in the takeover was about £50,000, of which fifteen thousand was set aside for the massive alterations to take place. The shareholders of the old Victoria Company were paid twenty-five shillings for each one pound share they held (at twenty shillings to the pound, this realised 25% appreciation); 65% of which was paid in cash, and the remainder was given in shares in the new company. Thus, the shareholders of the old company became shareholders in Odeon (Kettering) Ltd.

Work to transform the old building began immediately after closure. The balcony was completely dismantled and a new 'circle' erected. A new projection room was created in part of what had been the tearooms, and the old projection room area back stage removed.

The street front was completely swept away, breaking architectural unity with that side of Gold Street.

Typical newspaper publicity advert
for the Odeon, 1947
(Photo: Evening Telegraph (ET))

In its place was constructed an ultra-modern frontage, with tinted green, white and black tiling. Added was a modern canopy with letterbox, and a vertical fin with the word ODEON on both elevations. Above the canopy was a large decorative 36-pane window, which was illuminated at night. High above, striped tiling decorated the upper and the side, and a large ODEON sign was displayed on the side perspective which was neon-lit. It was a very imposing exterior and quite beautiful, giving a very modern look to Gold Street, even though it broke with conformity.

The entrance was full-width leading to two sets of entrance doors. Inside was a foyer with a central pay desk, a sales kiosk and display areas. The old corridor entrance to the stalls was blocked off and a new entrance into a holding area was created. Two sets of doors led left and right to the stalls. Washroom facilities for the stalls were accessed here. The circle was gained by stairs to the left of the entrance foyer, and these led to a 'crush area' where patrons queuing for circle seats could be held. Before the Second World War part of this area was used as a café. Entry to the circle was from another small foyer, which also provided access to washroom facilities and the door to the projection room.

The name's Bond – Derek Bond

A publicity photograph featuring the staff and manager, Derek Bond with obvious reference to a certain other Bond. (Photo: Evening Telegraph (ET))

The seating was increased to 740 in the stalls and 350 in the circle, however other figures suggest that the total seating was 1250. The interior décor was on ultra-modern lines, with the auditorium side walls curving gently towards the ante-proscenium of concave design, patterned with the sound and air apertures concluding at the wide proscenium which was architecturally lit.

The wide concave sweep of the ceiling from the proscenium included a lighting feature, providing the main illumination of the auditorium. This was repeated on each side wall.

It was planned to remove the large stage but records do not show this being done. Either way, the Odeon had a substantial stage area and an orchestra pit, and the dressing rooms were retained. The screen was on the back wall of the stage.

The Odeon in the 1950s (Photo: T. Smith)

The grand feature of the cinema was the great maroon front stage tabs (curtains) and the beautiful silk screen tabs with an embroidered scene of butterflies and flowers, an example of similar tabs to be found in many larger city Odeons. The main colour scheme throughout was predominantly shades of buff matched with doors in maroon, with other features picked out in cream and black. A later decoration, around 1951, provided a décor of shaded pinks and black doors outlined in cream. The Odeon was Kettering's first super-cinema, a modern delight, and the cinema-going public took to it at once.

The Odeon opened on Saturday, September 19th, 1936. On stage were local dignitaries, and the opening ceremony was performed by Mr. Steven Schilizzi MP. There then followed a prelude by Harry Pell's Premier Band. The film programme began with a cartoon, 'Robber Kitten', followed by Universal Talking News, and then 'Strike Me Pink' (1935), starring Eddie Cantor. The cinema foyer was ablaze with baskets of chrysanthemums, festooned with drapes. Seats had been fully booked days before.

The Odeon remained a popular cinema throughout its life. It was comfortable and luxurious. 1n 1954 a wide screen was installed, and new projection equipment replaced the BTH equipment that had been there since the days of the Victoria Picture House. Due to Cinemascope installation disputes, there was a period of loss of Twentieth Century Fox product, as had previously been the pattern. Many of the latest films were shown at the Odeon, however, with Paramount, another major distributor to Odeon, bringing out VistaVision – a new film process which required no major installation. Later Cinemascope, without the stereophonic sound system, became available and the Odeon installed its new 'Scope' screen.

From time to time concerts were staged, but the Odeon was foremost a cinema and many of the greatest films ever made had their first run in Kettering there. There was a world premiere when the cinema presented a charity showing of 'The Browning Version' (1951), starring Michael Redgrave and Jean Kent.

The Odeon had numerous managers during its life, each one contributing much to the success of the cinema – Messrs. Cooke,

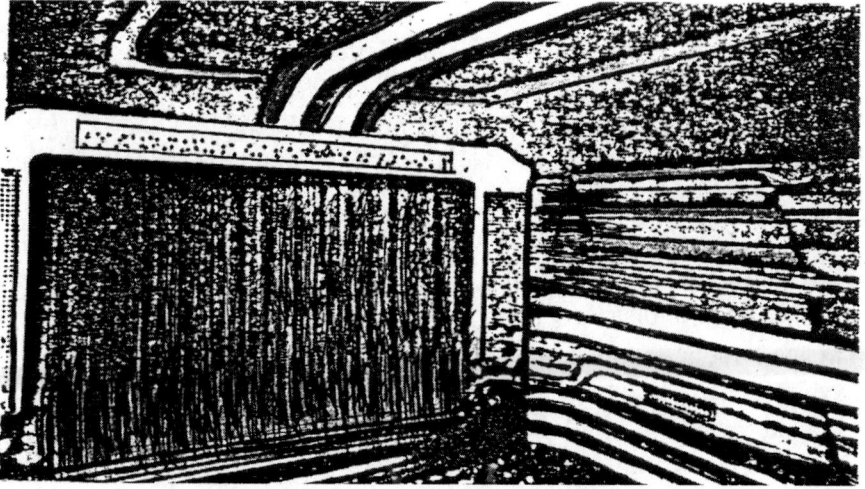

Artists impression of the ODEON auditorium

Shepheard, Brett and Barlow, to name a few; but none more so, perhaps, than Bert Dawson, who was the essence of a cinema manager and to whom I refer later.

My recollections of the Odeon are of class and comfort. It obviously followed the standard set by its predecessor. I first visited the Odeon one late afternoon with my aunt to see 'Pennies From Heaven (1936). I was just seven at the time. I remember little of the film but I do remember entering the cinema and experiencing the warmth of the atmosphere. It always seemed different to the other cinemas. They all had their own 'feel', but the Odeon was class. If you went to the matinee, you were 'treated' to twenty minutes or so of Victor Sylvester music playing the tunes of the day before the start of the show.(a popular broadcasting dance band of the time).When I occasionally hear his music today, my thoughts always go back to the Odeon.

It was always a busy cinema, especially on a Saturday night. To be sure of even getting in for the last complete performance, usually starting around 7.20pm, one would need to join the queue threading its way down the rear of Bakehouse Hill by six o'clock. The Commissionaire walked miles as he constantly traversed the queue, which often stretched along Lower Street, calling for singles or doubles at the seat prices offered as they became available.

Little wonder then that the announcement of closure was met with dismay in the town. Like all cinemas, it was suffering cinema-going decline but it was still a popular venue. The final week, the film showing was 'There Was A Crooked Man' (1960), starring Norman Wisdom. It was a good knockabout comedy and fitting, as it was such a film with which the Odeon had opened thirty-four years earlier. On Saturday, October 29th, 1960 the Odeon closed its doors for the last time as a cinema.

Fourteen months after closure, the building re-opened as a bingo hall. This was not particularly successful, but it remained on bingo for a little over ten years, finally closing in 1972. The building was demolished to make way for what is now part of the Newborough Centre. I remember at the time that there was much opposition to demolition by the townspeople, and many wanted to see the building taken up by the Borough Council and used as a much needed Civic Theatre. Alas the faint heart lost the fair lady and the lovely old Odeon, and seventy-two years of entertainment on the site, was to go forever.

Projection and Technical Information

The projection room was re-sited to a new room at the rear of the circle. It was equipped with two British Thompson-Houston (BTH) projectors fitted with BTH sound heads. The amplification and sound system was BTH. Speakers were contained in a special sound chamber constructed behind the stage back wall.

Around 1954 the projectors were replaced with Kalee 21s. It is not clear whether the sound system was changed, but I do recollect seeing Western Electric amplifier racks on my visits to the projection room in the mid-50s. Projectormatic was also installed. For anamorphic presentation, Delrama prismatic units were fitted to the Kalee 21s. The original screen installed in 1936 was on the back wall and a standard Academy ratio of 1:33 to 1. This screen remained until 1954 when a new multi-ratio screen was installed, with side variable masking making possible aspect ratios from 1:75 to 1 out to Cinemascope ratio of 2:35 to 1.

The Avenue Theatre

The townspeople were not slow in showing their delight in having a comfortable theatre. It was Thomas Payne who opened the first theatre, a gaff, in Kettering. At first it was portable theatre erected for visiting shows. Later, a permanent theatre was erected by him in Field Street and became known as the 'penny gaff'. Thomas Payne had two sons, William and Frank. William (W.J. Payne, Builders) had acquired land in Russell Street to build houses and had laid the foundations. It was early 1902 and the theatrical activities at both the Corn Market Hall and the Victoria Hall had put paid to the 'penny gaff'. Instead of houses, the brothers decided to build a permanent theatre; the sole proprietor being Frank Payne.

It was a fine theatre for a town the size of Kettering in those days, and unlike the Victoria Hall was designed and built for the express purpose of providing stage presentations. The building was a strange design, as its length was built parallel to Russell Street which resulted in a vast wall which was not particularly attractive, but it proved to be a blessing later in the theatre's life. The entrance was not on the street but via an opening leading off at ninety degrees from the street at the western end.

Mention is made in David Bradshaws's descriptive article, *My Technicolour Boulevard,* of two large wooden gates, not unlike factory gates, closing across this access. It is possible they were put in place when the theatre was built. It gave the building, however, a perspective of being somewhat like a large factory, but this was soon dispelled as one entered the theatre.

The entrance foyer contained the pay box each side of which a set of stairs took patrons to the balcony. Beyond the pay box was a wide corridor to the left which ran the length of the auditorium, thus parallel to Russell Street. From this corridor, access to the stalls was made through sets of doors. The seating was comfortable, those in the balcony priced at 6d. for the covered ones, and 9d. for the plush ones. The stalls were 2d., 4d., 6d. and 9d., with seats of plush upholstery to others with none at all. The capacity was around 800 overall.

The stage was large, measuring some 22 feet wide, 20 feet high and 30 feet deep (approx. 7m x 6.5mm x 9.5mm). The proscenium was constructed mostly of wood and canvas and the illumination by the latest electric lighting. The drop curtain was of a Northumbrian castle scene.

The theatre was filled to capacity on the opening night of Bank Holiday Monday August 3rd, 1903, the dignitaries taking all the 'posh' seats in the front stalls and balcony. Every seat in the house was filled for the opening show, which was to be one of the most outstanding of its kind and the likes of which had never been seen in Kettering. The opening week was a feast of opera by the Neilson English Grand Opera Company, who performed Gounod's *Faust* on the opening night, to resounding applause. The audience joined in the popular choruses during the finale, and the same was to be repeated throughout the week.

The reviews in the evening paper were full of praise for the new theatre:

AVENUE THEATRE
RUSSELL STREET · KETTERING
Prop. F. PAYNE

GRAND OPENING
BANK HOLIDAY MONDAY AUGUST 3RD. 1903

SPECIAL VISIT OF

THE NEILSON ENGLISH GRAND OPERA CO.
PERFORMING

FAUST
(GOUNOD)

PROGRAMME FOR THE WEEK

Tuesday August 4th.	**MARITANA**
Wednesday August 5th.	**LILLY OF KILLARNEY**
Thursday August 6th.	**TANNHAUSER**
Friday August 7th	**I'L TRAVATORE**
Saturday August 8th.	**DAUGHTERS OF THE REGIMENT**

Seats   STALLS 2d. 4d. 6d. 9d.   BALCONY 6d. & 9d.

7 o'clock each evening

Reproduction of the opening programme (Photo: M. Thornton)

Amid every sign of enthusiasm for its future success the curtain was rung up for the first time on the stage of the new Avenue Theatre in Kettering last night when a capital performance of 'Faust' was given by the Neilson English Grand Opera Company. The interior of the theatre presents a cosy appearance, the comfortable stalls being occupied by the prominent townspeople who were not slow in showing their appreciation in having a comfortable theatre in their midst. The effective drop scene painted by Mr. A. Maude depicting Alnwich Castle was duly admired and the orchestra, having tuned up the said curtain rose on the full company of artistes who were ready to perform. The orchestra struck up with the National Anthem and a few minutes later the curtain rose again to find Faust mourning his lost youth and the opening of Gounod's most famous opera was in full swing.

Thus it was to continue, as the Avenue presented a varied variety of stage entertainment through the years. There is little mention of cinematograph showings, though Bioscopes must have visited. An advertisement found for a week in September 1908, spoke of a presentation of 'animated pictures' by the St. Lawrence Picture Company, but no details of programme. In November 1908 the theatre closed and a few weeks later was reopened as a skating rink by a business syndicate named the Kettering Rink Company. It was not a great success, however, and lasted just two years as the **Rollerdrome**. In October 1910 it was closed again and reverted to a theatre.

The Coliseum – New Coliseum

'Have you seen the pictures and variety at the Kettering Coliseum? This week they are good. Next week they will be even better. Our pictures cannot be beaten – equalled – but not beaten.'

So ran the challenge in the advertisement for the week of November 7th, 1910. After the unsuccessful skating rink venture, the premises had reopened as a theatre for variety and pictures. It had a new name. The **Coliseum.**

During the twenty-three months as a skating rink, picture entertainment in the town had taken off with outstanding popularity. The

Victoria Hall was providing plays and 'living pictures'. Leo Vint had opened the Electric Palace, with the popular Arthur Brogden in charge and, with the Avenue no longer in competition with stage performances, he had full rein. Pictures were an important part of the programming of the Electric Palace, but it was not a large venue and there was room for some enterprise of a similar nature. So with new lessees and a new name, the Coliseum was about to do battle and take the high ground. That challenge in the opening week fired the first salvo.

The theatre had been leased to Jack Maynard and O.P. Drever Jnr. The first general manager was William Jackson, who in service during the Boer War had been mentioned in dispatches for rescuing his Sergeant under fire, after the man had been seriously wounded. With this background as his spur, he made some dramatic changes to the theatre.

The interior of the theatre was completely redecorated and reseated throughout, with plush tip-up seats. The stage was rebuilt and had splendid painted scenery and proscenium decoration. A projection box was installed at the rear of the stalls and lined with asbestos. One projector was installed. The outside of the theatre was enhanced with powerful electric lighting. A news report from the *Evening Telegraph* perhaps describes the change more significantly, under a heading *Pictures and Song* and dated 10th, November.

The Avenue in Russell Street has suffered many vicissitudes during its years of existence but it seems now to have permanently disappeared in that character and re-appeared under the guise of the Kettering Coliseum, a picture palace of the most up-to-date kind.

Jackman employed a full orchestra to accompany the singing and dancing, to play interludes, and for the pictures; an improvement it was said, on the lone piano hitherto. He provided popular and high class variety and he personally picked the films shown. This was noted in the report of the opening night that *films picked by Mr. Jackman include some of the most beautiful coloured pictures besides a complete range of interesting stories which are thrown on the screen by one of the most powerful electric machines made and which shows practically no flicker at all.*

The opening night was on Monday, 7th November, 1910 with a programme including 'All the Latest Pictures and Variety'. No details were reported, however the programme for the following week headlining 'The Maximillian Trio – jugglers, Alexander Mee with special song scena, and Carrie and Moore – American comedians and soft shoe dancers'. On the screen were 'All the Latest Pictures'. Seat prices were Pit 3d., Back Pit 2d., Orchestra stalls 6d., Balcony 6d. Business was excellent, with full houses nightly.

NUL SECUNDUS

THE **KETTERING COLISEUM**
(LATE AVENUE THEATRE)

ALL THE LATEST PICTURES AND VARIETY
Have you seen the pictures and variety at the Kettering Coliseum?
This week they are good • Next week they will be better
Our pictures cannot be beaten – equalled but not beaten

Next Week
Variety **THE MAXIMILIAN TRIO** Jugglers
ALEXANDER MEE Special song scena
CARRIE AND **MOORE**
American comedians and soft shoe dancers
and
ALL THE LATEST PICTURES

Pit 3d. Back Pit 2d. Orchestra Stalls 6d. Balcony 6d.

Cine-Variety, 1910
fashion
(Photo M. Thornton)

The film performances were one-reelers (up to around 1000ft.) which ran between the various acts. Most pictures ran for about ten minutes and the story (if any) told within that one reel. About that time films were being produced which were longer, two-reelers or more, and were beginning to make their presence felt in the mixed programmes of stage and screen. They began to be shown as separate items of the programme in their own right.

By the spring of 1911 the theatre had changed hands again, with no reason given. Brothers Arthur and James Thompson took over the business, the former becoming General Manager. There is nothing recorded to indicate what happened to the former lessees or to Jackman, for that matter. Mr. Wilfred G. Sturman was appointed musical director of the pit orchestra at the same time.

The operation of the Coliseum continued in much the same pattern during the following years. It is thought that an additional projector was installed, enabling longer films to be shown without breaks, but the building remained very much a theatre. And through the years many famous stars were to tread its boards, including Harry Tate, 'Buffalo Bill' Cody, Gracie Fields (billed as Miss Grace Field), and many more.

The boast of having the best pictures in town was progressively delivered, as was evident for the week of 14th June, 1912 when the Coliseum was advertising on stage 'Atlas and Vulcana' – the most graceful athlete and the strongest lady living. Pictures on the screen included 'The Adventures of Tom Butler', and 'The Derby' (1912). There would seem to have been a spate of such acts that week, as the Electric Palace was advertising 'Whizzing the Whirl', which was a sporting novelty act, and on screen pictures including 'The Derby' (1912).

The Thompson Brothers remained the lessees for many years but towards the latter part of the 1920s the Coliseum was experiencing difficulties, and there were spasmodic closings and re-openings throughout the decade. This was due no doubt to the Electric Pavilion and the opening of the Victoria Picture House. In 1928 the death of Frank Payne, described as the builder and owner of the Coliseum, occurred and it was supposed that this was the reason for the closure the week of December 10th, 1928.

The usual advertisement in the entertainments page of the *Evening Telegraph* for the week of December 17th stated that the theatre was closed *'owing to a disappointment'*. For the week of 2nd July, 1929, a similar advertisement appeared again, with no apparent reason given.

The records are not clear as to whether the Coliseum was open between those dates or not. With the death of Frank Payne, the Coliseum was put up for sale by auction and from the following report in the Kettering Leader dated 31st May, 1929 it appears that the theatre was experiencing difficult times.

Kettering Coliseum reserve price not reached
The reserve price of the Kettering Coliseum was withdrawn at £2.950
when offered for sale at the Royal Hotel. The sale was due to the death
of the owner Mr. Frank Payne who built the theatre in 1903. About
twenty people were present. The first offer was for one thousand five
hundred pounds and the amount rose steadily by one hundred pound
bids to two hundred thousand, nine hundred pounds. An advance of
fifty pounds was secured and at this stage the auctioneer announced
that he must withdraw the property. The theatre holds 850 people and
is let at two hundred and fifty pounds per year to Messrs. Thompson
Brothers who have the option of continuing their tenancy until 1934.

Apart from closure in July 1929 for a short season, programmes seem to suggest that stage performances continued. There are no programmes including films. An anecdote concerns the week of 17th February, 1930 when the theatre was advertising 'Blackmail' with the rider, 'a play in three acts. Not the talkie but the real thing' (references to the Alfred Hitchcock first British 'talkie' 'Blackmail' (1929), already shown in Kettering).

The managing director at this time was Jack Sherwood, who hailed from Tipton in Staffordshire, and had married May Payne, the daughter of Frank Payne. On the 7th August, 1931 he took over control of the Coliseum. The circumstances under which this came about are unknown, but he made some important changes to the old theatre.

The Coliseum, and the Avenue before it, was listed as a music hall, which it never was, and the new director was to dispel that misnomer for all time. Within a year Sherwood had removed the old projection box from the rear stalls and built a new one behind the balcony wall. New projection equipment was installed and the building was wired for sound. Seating was renewed throughout with pink, plush tip-up seats. The interior was changed by upgrading the entrance and access to the auditorium. The prices were set as 6d., 9d., and 1 shilling for the stalls, and 1/6d. for the balcony.

Changes continued piecemeal with new stage lighting and new draperies fitted, and these improvements were continually visible to delight the patron on their visits. The refurbished theatre reopened under its new name on 3rd August, 1932 as the **New Coliseum,** with a play called 'The Bird In Hand'.

Jack and May Sherwood became a very popular couple about town. Sherwood brought many fine acts to the stage and these were interspersed with popular films of the day. The manager was Mr. Harold Jackson, who was a 'matinee idol' type, totally suited to the role he was to play in the theatre's success.

So it was then that the New Coliseum enjoyed popularity as an entertainment venue in the town, under dynamic new management. Stars of the stage and radio appeared on its vast stage, and on its screen the film stars delighted its patrons. However, on April 6th, 1937 the greatest drama ever to be played out at the theatre was to take place.

It was around four o'clock on that fateful morning that an engine driver, who worked for the LMS and was returning home after his shift, noticed a glow within the theatre. As he approached the building, he realised that it was on fire. Shortly afterwards there was a tremendous roar as the flames exploded through the roof, sending debris everywhere. One of the worst fires in the history of the town was raging. Prompt action to call the Fire Brigade was too late to save the theatre, and it was completely engulfed.

The fire had started at about 2.30am in the centre of the stalls, and was almost certainly caused by a carelessly discarded cigarette butt. At times the heat was so intense it cracked the windows of the houses opposite, and some of the residents' walls were so hot that fire hoses had to be played on them to prevent further conflagration. By daylight, the old, much loved theatre had gone. All that remained standing were two chimneys and the wall that fronted Russell Street.

This great wall, which had on occasions been the cause of criticism in the past, certainly saved the rows of back-to-back houses in the surrounding streets, containing the fire as it did and which now stood blackened in the fashion of a sentinel. At 9.30am the Fire Officer declared the remains of the building were unsafe and ordered their demolition. Hours later, all that remained of the old 'Col' was a vast smouldering heap of twisted metal and blackened rubble.

There were two brighter notes, however. Peter, the theatre cat, had

The stage area after the fire
(Photo: Evening Telegraph (ET))

The balcony area after the fire
(Photo: Evening Telegraph (ET))

escaped from the blaze, and the film programme survived. The pictures for the three-day booking were 'Three Wise Guys', both of which are long obscure, and the British Paramount News. Some 12,000 feet of film in all. Whilst the projection room was wrecked, the fire had not broken into it, no doubt because of the efficiency of the firefighters. Had it done so, there would likely to have been a massive explosion caused by the nitrate film within.

My recollections of the New Coliseum are few. I must have visited the place at one time as it was the closest cinema to where I lived, and there were children's matinees. I do dimly remember the long corridor and the entrance off Russell Street. I am sure we queued in that corridor and entered the auditorium by another way. Perhaps not, but I do have recollection of the fire.

At that time I lived in Lime Road, and I recall my parents calling me into their bedroom to witness the big red glow that was in the sky and sparks rising in the night air. In later years my father told me that my mother was wakened by a frightening noise and alerted him. Looking from their bedroom window, they saw the glow of the fire. Sensing something out of the ordinary was taking place, they woke me so that I should see it.

My father, inquisitive as always, quickly dressed and, taking to his bicycle, charged off toward the glow. As a shoe worker, he thought it was the shoe factory in St. Peter's Avenue, but as he got nearer he realised it was the 'old Col'. Later that day, along with others, I was able to get into Russell Street and witness the still smoking rubble and the cracked windows of the houses.

It was the explosion and the crashing of the roof that woke the whole neighbourhood. At times the heat was so intense people living the houses opposite could not enter their front rooms for fear of their safety. The windows were cracked and the paintwork on doors and frames blistered. Shreds of the theatre roof were found in Mill Road, two streets away, and in Victoria Street. Other debris was found nearly two miles from the site.

One resident of Russell Street spoke of the fire, saying that he was wakened at around a quarter to four in the morning to the sound of crackling, quite similar to rifle fire, and looking out from his window he saw flames shooting out of the Coliseum roof. *'I opened my window and shouted "fire-fire" and then saw two men running up the street to call the Fire Brigade from the telephone box. Three others were racing to Orsborn's garage, next to the theatre, to get the lorries and buses away.'*

Mrs. E. Bradshaw, who lived nearly opposite, told of the intensity of the heat and how the theatre resembled the inside of a furnace.

'My husband came up the passage (hall) but it so hot he was forced back. We managed to move things from our front room because the flames from across the street were threatening. The strange thing is that there was no smell from the fire.'

Harold Jackson had been called out by the Police and told that the Coliseum was on fire. His reaction was one of disbelief. His first thoughts were for Peter, the black cat which had been at the theatre since a kitten. He had been locked in the bar, as a mouse had been seen in there. When Harold arrived at the theatre, he broke a window in the bar and climbed in. The fire had not reached that part of the building, but the smoke prevented looking for the cat. However, he need not have worried as Peter was found later in the day.

After the fire, when the debris was being sifted, a picture of Stan Laurel and Oliver Hardy, was found untouched by fire or water, hanging on what was left of a dressing room wall. They seemed to be looking down at the ruins as if to be saying, 'here's another fine mess we've gotten into'. Further into the debris was the remains of the balcony with a solitary heating radiator hanging suspended by its feed pipes.

The sad loss of the 'old Col' was the end of an era, and it had a profound effect upon the population of the town, and to many beyond belief. The realism that an old friend had gone took time to register and the only recently installed up-to-date stage lighting had never even been used.

Projection and Technical Information
Coliseum
The projection 'box' was situated at the rear of the stalls and was asbestos-lined. The single projector was a silent Pathe Imperial. Later a second projector was installed to permit longer films to be shown, but the make of that one is not known. It is likely two projectors of the same manufacture may have been installed. The projectors were now motorised and carbon arc was used, though the make unknown. There was also a carbon arc sourced slide lantern.

New Coliseum
The projection 'box' at the rear of the stalls was removed and a new one built behind the rear balcony wall. Two KALEE 7 projectors were installed, with British Talking Pictures (BTP) optical sound heads and BTP amplification. Sound was installed with the 1932 refurbishment.

The screen was mounted on the stage back wall. Speaker horns were mounted behind the proscenium. The light source was by Vulcan carbon arc lamp. The usual slide lantern was installed. Three colour stage lighting was installed, supplying overhead battens and footlights to the stage. It was controlled by the lighting board and dimmers from the side stage (actors' left). The fire destroyed it before it could be used for stage shows, etc.

Savoy

With the Savoy has risen a great house of entertainment out of the ashes of the Coliseum - Carry on Kettering.

Saturday, May 21st, 1938 saw the third super cinema opened within two years. This time it was the SAVOY in Russell Street. This new cinema-theatre, as it was called, had risen from the ashes of the former New Coliseum – and what a fitting tribute the new building was.

It has to be admitted that the determination of its managing director, Jack Sherwood, and others to rebuild was exemplary, and provided the town with a continuance of fine entertainment on the site for many more years. It became the only one showing pictures in the centre of town after 1974.

The Savoy was designed by C. Edmund Wilford, of Leicester, and built by Leighton (Contractors), of London. From the start, as many local businesses as possible were employed in the construction. Sand for the plasterwork was supplied by the Kettering Sand and Gravel Company, the sanitary engineering was by A.G. Miller, timber was supplied by Luck and Andrew in Wellington Street, and decorative materials by the Montagu Wallpaper and Paint Company. Uniforms were manufactured by the Kettering Industrial Co-operative Society, all of them renowned Kettering firms.

The design was quite different to the original Coliseum. Because of the lay of the site, it was still necessary to run the length of the cinema parallel to Russell Street; but there the similarity ended. The cinema towered above the streets and factories, dwarfing the houses that surrounded it. The entrance was built directly off Russell Street and was through two sets of four double doors which led to the foyer.

To the immediate right was the pay desk and other services. To the left were two sets of entrance doors to the stalls. At the far end were the stairs up to the circle lounge. To the right of this lounge, double doors led up steps into the centre of the circle. Services, which included the manager's office, the washrooms and the door to the projection room, were all situated in the circle lounge.

Front cover of the souvenir opening programme

The Savoy under Star Cinemas ownership with both film and bingo in 1968
(Photo: Evening Telegraph (ET))

Only when seated was it possible to appreciate the excellence of the interior of the auditorium. Tasteful colours led the eye to the huge Grecian Garden murals each side of the proscenium, the 'clouds' of which extended to the frieze running the length of the auditorium ceiling. The proscenium opening was 42 feet wide and arched away each side into the wall murals and into the décor of the ceiling plasterwork. The proscenium extension was decorated with three artistic grilles, which were adorned with artwork depicting musical notes. The whole interior was modelled in relief plaster and mouldings decorated in soft tones and hues.

The seating capacity was 774 seats in the stalls and 357 in the circle, fitted out entirely with mottled plush, in such a way that you had a good view of the stage and screen no matter where you sat. The furnishings and fittings were by Gaumont British Furnishings Ltd.

The stage was 48 feet wide and 24 feet deep. There were seven dressing rooms and a separate one for the orchestra. Fittings, included trap doors and full stage lighting as well as a spacious orchestra pit.

Exterior work was in brick and all the services were contained on Russell Street which included, in addition to the new entrance, exit ways, the stage door, and the scenery dock entrance. There were few windows and what there were had ornate cast iron grilles. The canopy over the entrance included a letterbox and an array of neon lighting. Above the canopy, a large fin carried the word SAVOY, picked out in neon. Neon lighting was fitted to the cinema's outline. Such was the effect of the neon speeding across the building and around the fin, that the residents opposite used it to light up their front rooms.

The opening of the Savoy was an event of the year, second only to the celebrations later in the summer of the granting of Borough status to Kettering. Each dignitary and guest was presented with a special souvenir programme, in which Harold Jackson spoke of his pleasure of succeeding to the management of so splendid a cinema-theatre as the Savoy. He also spoke of his intention to provide patrons with the finest programmes that were available.

The opening ceremony started with the customary speeches by notable dignitaries, followed by the Chairman of the Kettering Council – soon to be the Borough Council – performing the official opening amongst fanfares and music, whereupon the first film programme began with a Pathetone Weekly (a magazine reel with musical interlude), followed by a Popeye cartoon, and then the feature film 'Big City' (1937), which starred Spencer Tracy and Louise Rainer. Seat prices in the new theatre were Stalls 6d., 9d., and 1 shilling. Circle 1/3d. Matinee prices were Stalls 4d. and 6d. and the circle 6d.

Councillor Walter Dyson, J.P., declaring open the new cinema
(Photo: Evening Telegraph (ET))

Outside, before the opening ceremony, Russell Street was a bustling scene with crowds of people waiting to enter or just milling around soaking up the atmosphere. Bathed in the changing colours from the neon lights, the scene was not unlike a Hollywood premiere right there in the heart of Kettering. So crowded was the street that those arriving by car were unable to reach the doors of the cinema, having to leave them streets away.

Jackson lived up to his pledge, and the following week there appeared on stage Troise and his Mandoliers, a top recording band of the decade. Shows straight from a London season were brought to the stage, including the spectacular 'Belle of New York' with the London cast. Along with popular films of the day, top line stage and radio stars were presented. During the Second World War some very famous names appeared. Reginald Foorte, a very popular broadcasting theatre organist, for the week of 8th January, 1940, bringing with him his Moller theatre organ – it was later to become the BBC theatre organ after the Corporation's organ was destroyed by enemy action. Harold Ramsey brought his famous electronic organ to the stage, an instrument few Kettering people had ever seen the likes of.

The auditorium featuring the murals and the proscenium
(Photo: M. Thornton)

There were many others, too. Arthur Askey, Tommy Trinder, Sandy Powell, Will Fyffe, George Robey, Ella Shields (performing her famous 'Burlington Bertie' act), Dickie Murdoch and the 'Happidrome' radio show cast, to be followed by Tommy Handley and the ITMA radio show, and so many more.

The circus also visited the theatre. Lord Sanger's Circus arrived for a week, bringing with him three very large elephants which were stabled in the Angel Hotel yard. The walk to the theatre for two performances daily were a spectacle for children and adults alike, and provided some of the best sets of rhubarb on the allotments for years. The elephants had arrived in town by the circus train, which drew crowds to the goods yard at the station.

When presenting pictures, the cinema would open Mondays to Saturdays at 5.45pm and run a continuous performance, with the main feature twice and the supporting feature once. The news, trailers and any shorts were run twice. Matinees were on Monday, Thursday and Saturday at 2.30pm, and then continuous to the end of the evening. Stage presentations were usually once nightly at 7.30pm, or twice at 6pm and 8.30pm. Matinees were on Thursday and Saturday at 2.30pm.

One special company which found a home in the Savoy was, of course, the Kettering Operatic Society. For many years it staged its superb amateur productions in the fine theatre setting. Later the Kettering Theatrical Society also performed on the Savoy stage, under the very professional direction of Gladys Risely.

In 1937 Jack Sherwood also took control of the Empire, and he ran both houses until 1944 when Clifton Cinemas circuit bought the Savoy. The sale did not, however, include the Empire and he continued to run that cinema.

Clifton Cinemas took over the Savoy on August 25th, 1944. During the following years the cinema-theatre continued quality stage and screen presentation. The Savoy had never been a 'first run' house and, apart from a few non-circuit released offerings, ran films that had already visited other cinemas in the town. Nevertheless, with its stage presentations, it provided good entertainment for the town.

For a few years the well remembered Sunday afternoon concerts proved very popular, and top popular dance bands of the era were presented. Ted Heath, Vic Lewis and Cyril Stapleton, to name a few, entertained packed houses. I well remember the Ted Heath concert. The audience would not let the band leave the stage and it ran over time considerably, and the evening patrons for the films were delayed for over an hour.

From 1948 until 1951, the winter seasons were taken over by the Northampton Repertory Company who, by billing the Savoy under its own name, presented weekly plays. Plays had a limited popularity, with Kettering audiences brought up on variety, but good houses were maintained. For plays the stage proscenium was drastically reduced in size, but one play which was well received was 'The Murder in the Red Barn'. The last play performed by the Company was 'The Winslow Boy', ending a week's run on Saturday, 21st October, 1951.

The following day there was a concert by Billy Ternant and his Orchestra, and then the Savoy closed for a while. In late November it was announced that the Savoy would reopen under its original name on December 24th, with the pantomime Red Riding Hood. The pantomime played the theatre for two weeks, followed at once by another, Cinderella. To complete the holiday entertainment, Robert Bros. Circus was booked for a week. From that point it seemed the Savoy was back in business.

The cinema-theatre was now managed by Maurice Lee, and the pattern seemed to be winter presentations of stage and screen with a pantomime every Christmas. The remaining months the Savoy was on film. Prices at this time were Front stalls 1 shilling, Rear stalls 1/3d. Rear circle 2shillings, and Front circle 2/9d. For stage shows, the average price ranged from 2/6d. to 4/6d.

Personal recollections of the Savoy revolve mainly around the stage presentations, particularly during WW2. I liked the Savoy. It was a fine modern theatre and equal to many London houses, which of course were much too expensive to visit. I remember the visit of Reginald Foorte and his Moller organ. During the show the curtains were opened to reveal the 'works' of this massive instrument assembled on the stage, and taking up almost all of it.

Then there was the time, as a pupil, I was taken to a performance by the wartime London Philharmonic Orchestra, which wakened my liking for popular classical music. A few years on and it was the band shows. As far as the screen was concerned, my memories of the Savoy are very much the 1950s science fiction pictures. I think it must have shown all of them.

A wartime treat for the dark days of conflict (Photo: M. Thornton)

I was to have the privilege of working on the Savoy stage as a stage-hand with the Kettering Theatrical Society. One of their shows stands out as a classic memory. One evening, during a week's run of 'Kismet', one of the stays that supported the eighteen foot high scenery flats came adrift and, with the other stage-hands, I had to hold it upright for twenty minutes or so whilst the scene was played out on stage. The obvious wavering of the scenery must have amused many that night.

In 1967 The Star cinema circuit, of Leeds, acquired the Savoy. By that time bingo had been introduced alongside the film and stage shows, and remained a bedfellow until Sunday, February 25th, 1968, on which day the matinee performance of 'Bonnie and Clyde' (1967) became the last film to be shown in the original Savoy. That evening bingo was played as usual and at ten o'clock the cinema-theatre shut its doors, bringing an era to a close.

The theatre underwent extensive alterations, converting the former stalls into a bingo facility, and transforming and extending the circle into

A Savoy 'scoop'?
(Photo: Evening Telegraph (ET))

a first floor luxury cinema with seating for 465, complimenting ultra-modern furnishing and décor. It was this transformation that hid the glorious décor of the old Savoy forever.

The official opening of the new Savoy took place on Monday, September 9th, 1968, with the film, 'Charge of the Light Brigade' (1968), starring Trevor Howard and John Gielgud, who sent tributes to the reception. Relics of that famous charge were displayed, including the preserved head of Roland, the horse ridden by the Earl of Cardigan at the Charge, as well as the Lancers' original helmet.

The reception was at the Royal Hotel and the dignitaries and guests were escorted to the Savoy by four horsemen dressed as Lancers. Vehicles of the 108th Recovery Regiment (TA) escorted the mayoral car. Crowds waiting in Russell Street were reminiscent of the opening of the Savoy thirty years earlier. Many were turned away that night as the refurbished cinema quickly filled and the first performance began. As for the ground floor, it received some refurbishment and was fitted out for permanent bingo operation.

The Savoy continued operations in this way until Saturday, September 7th, 1973, when it was closed once more for even further conversion, this time to a twinned studio-style cinema. The last film to show was 'Lady Caroline Lamb' (1972), starring Vera Miles and Jon Finch. This was the last of the Savoy, for it was to change dramatically. For those who remember it and for the record, it was a sad change for the old Savoy held favour for many in its years since 1938. Sadly, the shell was still standing when I last visited, derelict and forlorn. Surely the old place deserved a better fate and, as a past resident of the town, it disturbed me profoundly.

Projection and Technical Information
The Savoy was well equipped for both pictures and stage. The projection installed when the Savoy was built is obscure but is thought to be KALEE 7s or 8s. The arc lamps were Kalee Vulcan. Sound heads were British Talking Picture and the sound system British Acoustic. In 1955 the sound system was RCA and the projectors thought to be Ross FC or GC, an easy conversion for wide screen formats. When Cinemascope was installed, the arc lamps became Peerless. The anamorphic lenses were Kalee Varamorph. The stage was 48feet wide and 24ft. deep. Stage lighting controls were back stage (actors' left) and the fly tower operation was actors' right. Follow spots were situated in the projection room. A Cinemascope screen was installed and could be 'flown'. The Savoy was fitted with an Ardente Hearing system to assist patrons with hearing difficulties, and in the early days could be used as a paging service for doctors, etc.

The Studios – Ohio Cinemas
The Studio cinemas were created within the first floor of the theatre. The bingo facility was retained on the ground floor. By this time, the Granada was the only other cinema open in the town. In the early 1970s it was the trend to carve up auditoria in large cinemas to create smaller studio-type cinemas, and a similar development befell the old Savoy circle under the Star cinemas banner, though fortunately the screens were a respectable size in relation to the auditoriums created.

The conversion was accomplished within twelve days and consisted of a dividing wall lengthways through the existing circle area, giving an almost equal dimension to the two cinemas. The wall was supposedly fully sound insulated, but one could detect a slight seepage of sound, one to the other, particularly during very loud passages on soundtracks. Contrasting colour schemes were introduced and wall-to-wall carpeting gave a bright and modern look to the studio-style cinemas. Both were fitted with psychedelic lighting effects. The projection room remained unaltered except for additional projection ports, and served the two screens with single system projection systems.

The 'twins' opened on Friday, April 20th, 1973. Studio One presented 'The Ten Commandments' (1956), starring Charlton Heston and Yul Brynner, while Studio Two opened with 'Cabaret', starring Lisa Minnelli and Michael York. The whole complex, comprising of the cinemas and bingo, took on the title of the Kettering Entertainment Centre. EMI acquired the Centre a few years later and subsequently closed the bingo operation, but the Star Group held the lease for the cinemas and continued to operate them.

Conversion and re-naming to Studios 1 & 2
(Photo: M. Thornton)

Hamblin Leisure, a county-based company, took over the whole building and re-opened the bingo operation, with Star continuing the lease and operating the cinemas.

On January 24th, 1985, the twin cinemas closed. According to the Star Group, the cinemas had been losing money for some time. The Manageress Margaret Osborne and Alan Gray, the projectionist, lost their jobs along with eight other staff. The bingo continued to operate, however. The last films to show were 'Gremlins' (1984), along with an 'olde tyme' show which featured two silent shorts, one of which was 'Barefoot Boy' (1910). Included in the show was an organ interlude performed by 68-year-old George Tingle on an electronic instrument. An amusing anecdote to this last performance was that as 'Barefoot Boy' was being projected, it started to rip apart, but skilful work by the projectionists assembled hand-cranked the film through the projector. (It is not clear what projector was used for this operation – possibly a Kalee.)

Publicity for the opening of the twinning of the cinema
(Photo: Evening Telegraph (ET))

Over two hundred people were turned away that night and, in a poignant speech, Alan Gray said, *if you lot had turned up in the past we wouldn't have been closing down tonight.*

With the Granada now long turned over to bingo and the Studios closed, Kettering had no cinema and motion-picture performances ceased after eighty-eight years. Films did return, however.

It was Easter 1986 when the old theatre site was to see film returned to the darkened screens. Mr. Ashley-Whyatt leased the two cinemas and undertook a programme of refurbishment. At first, only Screen One was brought back into use and it opened with a matinee performance of 'Return to Oz' (1985), an odd choice to reopen with as it was a much-to-be-desired up-date of a children's favourite. However a goodly number of patrons had to be turned away as the 140 seats in the screen soon filled. Screen Two opened shortly afterwards and just as unceremoniously.

Studio One. Half of the circle area now divided (Photo: Kettering Museum)

The screen in Studio One. Note the lack of screen masking (Photo: Kettering Museum)

Ashley-Whyatt was known for his cinema operations locally, as he already ran the Forum in Corby and the newly-activated Electric Palace at Burton Latimer, formerly known as Bentleys. The Kettering cinemas were given a new name and, taking the name of its twin town in the U.S.A., became the OHIO CINEMAS, which incidentally was the name also applied to the Burton Latimer cinema.

When work was fully completed, new heating to both auditoria had been fitted, some new seating, new foyer lighting and decoration, and updated projection equipment installed.

The success hoped for was to last only a few years and by the end of the decade both cinemas had become less popular, with many people, particularly the young, preferring to travel to the multiplex at Milton Keynes than frequent the progressively shabby Kettering screens. So closure was on the cards once more.

In 1990 Brian McFarlane took over the Ohios and he began a programme of further refurbishment, again re-equipping with the latest in projection equipment and sound systems. Retaining the OHIO banner, he began with Screen Two, re-seating it with 160 to a high standard, which presented a cosy and comfortable auditoria with an acceptable-sized screen. The sound system was updated to full Dolby surround, and changed its name to **Ohio 1**. The remaining screen (originally One) also received 140 new seats and new Dolby stereophonic sound.

Both screens were programmed to run two shows nightly, with extra matinee shows during holiday times. A whole range of films to cater for all tastes

OHIO CINEMAS
RUSSELL STREET, KETTERING
TELEPHONE 0536 515130

MOVIES SHOWING FROM FRIDAY
19th MARCH TO THURSDAY 25th MARCH

UNDER SIEGE (15)
with STEVEN SEAGAL
7.30pm Nightly

RESERVOIR DOGS (18)
9.20pm nightly

THE BODYGUARD (15)
with
KEVIN COSTNER and WHITNEY HOUSTON
9pm Nightly

HELLRAISER III (18)
7.30pm Nightly

HOME ALONE 2 (PG)
Matinees only Saturday 3pm, Sunday 3.30pm

HONEY, I BLEW UP THE KID (U)
Matinees only Saturday 3pm, Sunday 3.30pm

AFTERNOONS £1.80 AND EVENINGS £2.00

OHIO CINEMAS
RUSSELL STREET, KETTERING ☎ 515130
MOVIES SHOWING FROM FRIDAY 14th FEBRUARY

THE ADDAMS FAMILY (PG)
Fri 5pm & 9.15pm. Sat 3pm, 5pm & 9.15pm
Sun 4pm & 9.15pm. Mon-Thurs 3pm, 5pm & 9.15pm

FREDDIES DEAD
The Final Nightmare (18) 7.30pm & 9.15pm

BILL & TEDS BOGUS JOURNEY (PG) 7.30pm

AN AMERICAN TAIL 2 (U)
Sat 3pm, Sun 4pm, Mon-Thurs 3pm
ALL SEATS £1.70

Ohio publicity for February 1992 (Photo: Evening Telegraph (ET))

were screened, utilising the two screens at different times of the day and evening, and this worked well until 1996 when the situation again became serious.

Brian confessed to me that he did not know how much longer he could continue. On the evening I visited, two weeks before Christmas, there were just two patrons in Ohio 1, and Ohio 2 had not opened. His dilemma was beyond his ability to escape. Because of low returns, he could not book the latest releases and he only had a few supporters backing his efforts. There would be some respite over the holiday period, but what then? Eight months later the Ohios had closed. It was the Granada and the Empire all over again. In a population of over 50,000, only two people could be bothered to turn out to see a cracking film.

A sad end to the once proud Savoy. The precious wonderful stage now moribund, converted to the worship of gambling, the ghosts of the past great stars still lurking within its walls. The hallowed interior given over to seats where people sit pinning their hopes and wealth on the luck of a set of numbers, with little knowledge or care for the hallowed place they occupy.

Closed and forgotten. The cinema building in 1999
(Photo: M. Thornton)

Hidden from view is the graciously adorned interior, now decayed and peeling. The once pleasant foyer, its atmosphere of excitement and anticipation for what was to come, now just an empty space.

In this building and on this site, nearly one hundred years of entertainment had delighted its patrons. Then the townspeople loved it. Now it is dark, derelict and un-loved, open to vandals and graffiti louts who burgle and plunder with no interest in its past glory. Its fate still remains in the balance and the building still stands derelict. There is an application for planning to demolish the building and erect a residential development of one bedroom flats. The decision is expected in 2013, meanwhile the old Savoy stands defiantly.

Projection dating from the latter years. Single system with film feed from a tower seems to be the installation here with the top box cut away. (Photo: M. Thornton)

Projection and Technical Information

Studios

2 Ross GC3 projectors (one for each screen) fitted with Radio Corporation of America (RCA) soundheads and with RCA amplification Xenon light source and Kalee Variomorf anamorphic lenses for each projector. At some time Kalee 21 projectors were fitted, thought to be prior to 1989.

Ohios
Screen 1 (ex screen 2) Kalee 21 projector with RCA amplification Tower
feed and retrieval system
Later: Dolby and Stereophonic sound installed
Xenon light source
Screen 2 (ex Screen 1)
Until 1989 Ross GC3 projector with RCA soundhead and amplification
From 1989 Kalee 21 projector with RCA soundhead and amplification
From 1995 Monee Projector with Dolby sound
Xenon light source

Kettering Electric Pavilion – Gaumont Pavilion

The Kettering Electric Pavilion to give its full name, or the Pav as it
was fondly called, was the town's first purpose-built cinema, the first
to run continuous performances, the first to show 'talkie' features. It
was foremost in the showing of British films, most of them reaching its
screen at one time or another.

The Pav changed very little in its lifetime, both structurally and
architecturally. The frontage remained right up until 1953 and today,
had it survived in its original style, it surely would have been a listed
building. Sadly, like many of its kind, it has gone and is a hazy
memory.

Around 1912 the only venues for motion-pictures were Vints Palace,
The New Avenue and the Victoria Hall. Variety, plays, and other stage
presentations were their core business, and 'living pictures' were fill-
ins. As is known, travelling Bioscopes brought pictures to the local
halls.

There was room for a new enterprise in Kettering, and surprisingly
it came from outside of the town. At the end of the High Street, close to
Bakehouse Hill and only a few yards from the Victoria Hall, the site on
which the residence of Mr. John Newman stood came onto the market
in 1912. It was bought by the Rotherham Electric Theatre Company.
Demolition took place and construction started almost immediately
on what was advertised as a new Picture House, in keeping with the
importance of the town.

Kettering's first purpose-built cinema
(Photo: D. Wharton)

It was named the Kettering Electric Pavilion and opened at 5.30pm on Saturday, May 10th, 1913. The first screening was at 6pm and then was continuous until 10.45pm. The programme was 'When Lee Surrendered', 'Interrupted Honeymoon', 'On Account Of a Transfer' and 'Fog'. Prices were: front seats 2d., centre 4d., and rear seats 9d. The cinema was an immediate success. People liked the new-found freedom of being able to walk up at any time they wished.

The report of the opening spoke of *'a new, brightly-lit palace for the pictures, a welcome addition to Kettering's wealth of entertainment. The pictures are clear and well exhibited in a building specially designed for them. It is comfortable and airy, and one can walk up virtually at any time and is usually assured of a seat. Its very name swells the breast with pride and so it should.'*

The Pavilion soon lost its proud title, and became simply the Electric Pavilion, or 'Pav'. The cinema could seat 650 in a single auditorium with no balcony. In the original plans, one was to be constructed later. Why this was so, is not clear. Perhaps the money ran out or was not forthcoming, who knows? But the balcony was never built, probably due in the end to the intervention of the First World War the following year. A raked floor was provided and patrons could see the screen comfortably – that is, if you did not sit in the front rows.

While the interior was comfortable, it did not live up to the more classic architecture of the exterior. The entrance was by six marble steps leading into the vestibule, and up to the central pay box. Either side of the entrance were two tall circular pillars supporting the upper masonry. On each side of the entrance were shop fronts, to the left the cinema office, storage and circular stairs to the projection room. On the right the shop was occupied by a hairdresser and milliner. In later years this also became an area used by the cinema.

On the upper fascia there were three ornate panels, each with a small window on each side. On these panels were inscribed KETTERING ELECTRIC PAVILION. Above the central panel rose a Gothic-style arch with a lunette drop window, which was the projection room. Above the other two panels were parapets. Centrally on the roof was a small tower which formed the ventilation system, and on top of the tower was a decorative globe, which was lit at night, and a flag pole.

Along the front of the building hung four, very large, electric globe lights and the stonework was illuminated by forty-eight electric lamps. It is no wonder that it was named the Electric Pavilion, for these lights bathed the High Street and the whole of Bakehouse Hill in a blaze of illumination not to be found anywhere else in the town.

Entrance to the auditorium was by two sets of very large and heavy doors each side of the pay desk, though I can only remember going through the left hand set. Once inside, big heavy curtains were encountered, making a light trap. Later doors were also fitted which created a cave-like space between the two sets of doors. I remember as a boy tugging open these huge doors and, as they closed after me, being engulfed in near total darkness while negotiating the second door, and made even worse by going in out of the daylight.

The interior was described at the time as comfortable but modest, and that it certainly was. The walls of the hall were plainly decorated. Every few feet, buttresses rose from the floor to the roof, and served as supports for the girder-work of the roof. In between were ventilation shafts. At the top of the walls ran a plasterwork frieze and a false parapet. There was no false ceiling and the girders supporting the roof were visible.

The cinema had no stage to talk of. The proscenium was modelled on the style of a Roman Pavilion, with an arch and fluted columns. Plaster-worked scrolls and ornamental cherubs filled the arch. The proscenium arch had a marble effect and the flutes were in gilt. The screen tabs were golden in colour to match. The stage was quite high and of moderate width. The front was patterned canvass-covered, which was illuminated when the house lights were lit. After the silent picture days, the sound non-sync equipment was under the stage and the canvas decoration was retained. At one time the tabs may have been opened from there, too. The screen was on the back wall. To the left of the small stage were a set of wooden steps, and on the right an exit which led directly into Wadcroft.

There was no cross gangway at the rear of the stalls, nor midway. There were two aisles each side, with seating right up to the side walls. The toilet facilities were off the right side of the auditorium, and anyone sitting left of centre or in the left hand block of seats was required to walk down to the front, along by the stage, and halfway up the right aisle, to reach them. The Pavilion was quite steeply raked, which resulted either in a sprint or a climb for which direction one was going. The same problem arose for the sales assistant who always stood at the front, having got there safely after entering the cinema with her fully-loaded tray via the High Street and entrance doors. I digress, for those anecdotes apply to later years.

For Kettering, the new purpose-built cinema was luxury indeed and was very welcome. The opening was a grand occasion. During the silent era, music for the films was mostly played on a piano by Florence Martin, who had a mirror to assist her because of the high level of the screen. For prestige pictures, a fine little bijou orchestra augmented the piano, though where it, and the piano, was placed is unknown. In silent days it is thought the seating was not so close to the stage. There were also musical interludes by local musicians when important pictures were shown.

The Pav became the premier picture house until 1920, when the Victoria Picture House and the Empire came on the scene. Its advertising seems to have been almost entirely by handbill and poster. Few adverts appeared in the local paper for its programmes until the 1920s, and then because of the opposition, most likely. It showed all the popular films of the day and just about the whole repertoire of Chaplin films.

The cinema changed hands in 1919, Messrs Hutton and Shapiro taking control, but there was little change to the cinema in their time. And in 1927 it changed hands again when the Pav was bought by Denham (Midland) Cinemas Ltd. which was part of the Gaumont British Picture Corporation, and subsequently its name was changed to the **Gaumont Pavilion.**

In late 1929 the Gaumont Pavilion closed for a short time to be wired for sound. The 'talkies' had already found their way to Kettering with shorts – mainly musical or filmed variety acts exhibited at the Victoria Picture House – but feature films were yet to make their debut.

This was remedied on Monday, December 9th, 1929 with 'Perfect Alibi' (aka Alibi) 1929, and a supporting programme of a sound cartoon 'Oprey House' and a newsreel. The debut was a huge success and a review in the *Evening Telegraph* of the 10th December recorded:

Acquired by the Gaumont-British Picture Corp. the cinema was renamed Gaumont Pavilion and remained so until 1953 with little change (Photo: D. Wharton)

Successful Talkie at the Kettering Pavilion

Anyone who loves dramas without too much love interest and where the plot is compounded in a battle of wits rather than the endless competition of combats will find the ideal picture in 'Perfect Alibi,' a full 100% talking picture which will be showing all the week. The plot is easy to follow as is the dialogue. Supporting is a highly amusing sound cartoon 'Oprey House' and a silent comedy which relies on clever plot rather than ludicrous acting as entertainment. All together a good show bearing in mind that nothing is perfect during its trial run. The clarity of the talkie is praiseworthy.

Here a brief explanation is required, as it is with certainty that the Pavilion had been fitted out with both the Warner Bros. Vitaphone sound on disk system, and the optical sound track system (on the film). The Vitaphone disk system was the first to emerge in 1926 when Warner Bros introduced it with their film 'Don Juan' (1926), where they used synchronised sound for the musical sequences. In November 1927 'The Jazz Singer' was released as a part-talkie and is recognised as the beginning of talking pictures.

In January 1927, William Fox, having bought out the rights to an optical sound on film, patent launched the system which he called Movietone, but in essence it was the Radio Corporation of America which was responsible for Photophone sound on film which employed photographed (optical) sound. Films were being made with both sound systems into the 1930s, when by international agreement sound-on-film was declared the sound system for films, and by that time the disk system was almost extinct.

What has this to do with the Electric Pavilion? The film 'Perfect Alibi', which gave the cinema its talkie debut, was written and directed by Roland West for United Artists. U.A. was part of a group of studios who had agreements with Western Electric subsidiary, ERPI, who were marketing a sound-on-film system. The newsreel was an early Movietone, a product of William Fox which began life the same year. The cartoon was sound-on-disk as was the supporting short not advertised.

This indicated, therefore, that the Pavilion was up-to-date and able to show films using both sound systems. There is no record the 'The Jazz Singer' was ever shown in Kettering, but the Pavilion ran the second part-talkie 'The Singing Fool' (1928), which also starred Al Jolson. The first full all-talking picture, 'Lights of New York' (1928), also graced the Pav. screen.

The Gaumont Pavilion continued to be a major house in the town for many years and well into the 1950s. I remember the old Pav well, because that was where I got to see one of my favourite female stars, Shirley Temple. One scene from 'Captain January' (1936) was my own favourite. This story of a shipwrecked little girl was special for me, as in one scene she walks towards a door, turns to the camera and winks. For this seven-year-old, that wink was for me. Ah! The magic of cinema.

By the 1950s, the Pav. was ageing. It had served well during the conflicts of WW and WW2, but there had been little change to its appearance internally or externally and its owners, by now the Rank Organisation, scheduled the old cinema for a complete refurbishment. The Gaumont Pavilion closed on the 2nd of September, 1953, the last film to show was 'Thunder Bay' (1953).

Forty years of pictures in its dark interior had come to a close, momentarily. It had seen and pioneered the great change from silent to sound. Never again would we see one of the projection staff slip through the sliding door of the stage just before the end of the feature, and out again after the start. Was it he who played selections of interval music from 'The White Horse Inn' and perhaps opened and closed the tabs? Or was it Archie Mason, slipping away from the box for a few minutes respite? We may never know.

Projection and Technical Information

In 1913 the projector was a single Ernemann mute machine and a slide lantern. There was need for a second machine and the Ernemann was replaced by two RUFFLES Bioscope projectors, which were manufactured in Northampton. They were replaced by two Gaumont Chronos and fitted with 'mirror lite' arc lamps, using 8inch mirrors. These projectors were replaced yet again by two Powers Camaragraph No. 6. In 1929 the installation of sound resulted in two Simplex

Standard projectors and Cinephone soundheads. A Vitaphone turntable was behind each projector with BTH head. Sound was Westrex. These projectors were replaced with two Gaumont 16s in the mid-30s with British Acoustic sound heads and amplification. Kalee Vulcan arc lamps provided the light source. It is thought that the projection equipment was upgraded at a later date but to what is obscure. Possibly Kalee 8s.

Refurbished in 1953 and renamed Gaumont
(Photo: Evening Telegraph (ET))

Gaumont
'Is it me or is it the cinema they have come to see?' Joan Collins

Within three weeks the old cinema had undergone a transformation, and Kettering picture-goers saw the old frontage disappear beneath a modern facade, to be lost from view for the next six years or so.

The upper part of the frontage was retained. The large panels with the name GAUMONT PAVILION disappeared, and GAUMONT was replaced on each panel. The shop fronts either side of the entrance were replaced by attractive brickwork, with entrances modernised. The old pillars each side of the entrance were encased with an attractive hardwood feature. Between them and above them, a canopy was created with down-lights illuminating the entrance. At the entrance, two sets of double doors were constructed with fanlights above.

Entrance to the cinema was still by the original six marble steps, which had been revamped in white mottled tile with black edge strips. The pay box was still in the centre but entrance to the cinema was now by doors on each side leading into a vestibule, which had been created and tastefully decorated with decorative lighting and publicity spaces. Once inside the auditorium, however, the changes were more dramatic.

Patrons could mingle in a new comfortable vestibule before entering the auditorium through two further sets of doors, which gave a luxurious sense to the cinema. The auditorium had been completely refurbished. The roof girder work had been completely encased with a false ceiling, dotted with spotlight down-lighters. New seating had been installed, reduced to 550, to accommodate the new vestibule. The toilets were completely rebuilt and modernised.

The most striking change was the proscenium. A modern, clean-lined proscenium arch was created which meant that the ornate plasterwork was removed, including the cherubs which were seemingly lost forever. (What lovely museum pieces they would have been!) The small stage was remodelled and a new wide screen installed which left very little of the original. The auditorium was decorated in soft shades and the ventilation shafts had been concealed beneath new walling. Deep carpet completed the new-found luxury of the cinema, but that rake remained – though seemingly not quite so steep.

The appearance of the cinema was very pleasing indeed, and I remember being quite impressed by its cosy atmosphere. New projection equipment was installed, as well as a new sound system. The new screen was an admirable size for the auditorium, giving a good clean shape to the projected picture whether widescreen or CinemaScope, and was awesome with VistaVision.

Patrons gave their approval when on the re-opening, they thronged the High Street and Bakehouse Hill to witness the event. On Friday evening, the 25th September, 1953, the refurbished **Gaumont** re-opened. What an occasion, and there were scenes reminiscent of the Regal and Savoy opening all those years ago.

Opening night of the refurbished Gaumont
(Photo: Evening Telegraph (ET))

To open their new cinema, Rank had sent along one of their top stars, Joan Collins. She was dressed like the movie queen she was, and adored by the crowds who had come to see her. The event was reported the following night.

The transformation of Kettering's oldest cinema into a luxurious palace of entertainment with the town's brightest screen was warmly applauded last night by an enthusiastic audience. Within the period of twenty one days residents had watched their oldest entertainment house having its face lifted. High stone steps and pokey pay box, shop windows and doors have been banished. Instead there stands a glittering new theatre on the structure of the old but streamlined. Cleverly decorated and brilliantly lit.

Joan Collins, 20 year old star of many British films arrived wearing a black sequined cocktail dress and white fur stole and her deep tan was evident of her return from location in Spain where she has just finished shooting her latest picture. Crowds lined the High Street on both sides filling the pavements. Such was the magnitude of the people that Miss Collins was heard to say 'is it me or the cinema they have come to see?' The Mayor in his opening address said 'this theatre has more than just luxury. It has tradition. We remember it as an old cinema when the slides were scratched with a pin and the Musical Director was a solitary pianist positioned beneath the screen. It speaks well for the entertainment at this house in that it has stood the test of time and is still with us today.' Miss Collins then received a pair of golden scissors and cut the massive tape draped across the screen and the first pictures in the re-modelled cinema began.

The opening programme was 'Genevieve' (1953), starring the popular quartet of Kay Walsh, John Gregson, Dinah Sheridan and Kenneth More. The support was 'Murder At 3am' (1947), starring Denis Price, and the current issue of the Gaumont-British News completed the programme. The tradition of showing British films was truly to be continued as the next film nine days later was 'Innocents In Paris' (1953), starring Alistair Sim and Margaret Rutherford.

I remember the opening night. I was working at the Granada at the time and Friday night was my night off. I milled around the High Street, soaking up the atmosphere. The Gaumont looked a picture all dressed up, and I felt a warm respect for the old place.

During its short life, the Gaumont provided good entertainment for its patrons. It was very much akin to the Odeon, sharing its newsreel and often its manager. There was once a small fire, but it caused little damage and did not even result in closure. Sadly the tradition of good entertainment could not save the Gaumont, and after only six years it was to close.

Notice of closure was given on October 3rd, 1959. The last show was 'Last Train From Gun Hill' (1959), starring Kirk Douglas and Anthony Quinn. The old picture house went out fighting and its doors closed for the final time at 10.45 on Saturday, 10th October, 1959 to a full house. For one person, it was the end of an era. The chief projectionist, Archie Mason, had shown pictures at the cinema most of his working life. Westerns were his favourite pictures. What a fitting, if sad, finale for Archie.

The End. After 46 years of cinema. The proscenium arch pillars of the first cinema can be seen. One wonders what the boys are thinking

The people of Kettering did not really understand what was happening, for it was just a year later when the Odeon also closed. Effectively the Rank Organisation had stopped showing pictures in Kettering, and it was not without reason that picture-goers felt bitter towards the company; and perhaps justifiably so.

The Gaumont was a popular cinema and though, like most, its audiences had dwindled, it was well used. Odeons and Gaumonts were closing throughout the country and market forces were in full flight. The Gaumont site was a financial property deal. Who wanted pictures when financial assets were for the grasping?

Projection and Technical Information

Two Gaumont-Kalee 21s with Westex Soundheads and Westrex Amplification Kalee President Arc Lamps.

Delrama anamorphic lenses were used for CinemaScope 'squeeze prints', it is understood.

Speakers behind the screen, the sound chamber accessed by the double steel doors on the back wall visible from Wadcroft.

Cinemascope was optical sound. VitaVision by 35mm.

Because of the long shape of the auditorium, good presentation of all ratios was possible.

Empire – New Empire

There will be few who can remember the Empire in Eskdail Street as it was. Today it is a car repair centre, and over the years successive owners have torn away the name 'EMPIRE CINEMA', which for many years remained proudly displayed on high even after its demise. Though little remains of the original frontage now – the needs of the motor car have taken care of that – one can still see one or two features of this little old cinema which had a special place in the cinema history of Kettering, and which was left deserted by the public when it needed them most.

It was late in 1919 when three enterprising businessmen laid plans and began the building of the town's second purpose-built cinema. Mr. H.G. Roughton, Mr. A Cheney and Mr. T. Bamford, who owned a photographic business in Montague Street, formed a company and acquired land a short distance into Eskdail Street.

The building was quite simple, being a basic hall with a pitched roof. The front was constructed out of brick and, with the exception of the entrance, was nondescript. The entrance, however, gave the cinema its architectural character. This was in the form of a grand arch, the buttresses constructed in stone rising to the first parapet and decorated with Roman-style regalia. The wide archway forming the entrance was ornately carved and the keystone bore an innominate crest.

Above the first parapet was an ornamental cornice and a small aperture, the projection room window, each side of which 'EMPIRE CINEMA' was inscribed in bold Roman lettering. A second parapet ran across the very top, on which there were three decorative roundels. In early days each roundel supported an electric ornamental globe. On each side of the entrance were small windows side by side, three higher up the brickwork and two below. Later a fin was built onto the right hand of the front, with the word 'EMPIRE' in neon on both sides.

An impression of how the Empire looked. No actual photographs have been discovered of the early period

Its outward appearance was typical of the smaller, modest, purpose-built cinema of the day, where in most towns you could usually find at least one. Many of them were destined to become 'flea pits' or 'bug hutches' in later years, but the Empire could never have been in that category.

Internally it was an intimate modest, comfortable cinema. Entering, the central pay box was gained in three short steps. Each side were two double doors leading into a small light-trap vestibule, which ran the width of the cinema with stairs to the balcony leading from both left and right sides. It was small but enabled access to the pay box, toilets and a small door, on the other side of which there was a vertical iron ladder leading up to the projection room. The stalls were gained by double doors either side, serving the left and right aisles. The crimson-coloured walls were relieved by panels of white and cream, and quaint electric lamps were set in them. The seating was red plush tip-up and the floor raked.

Publicity for August 1920

The Empire opened on Monday, May 3rd, 1920 with 'Still Alarm' (1919), starring Jack Manley and Betty Fordham, which ran Monday through to Saturday. The supporting programme, however, changed midweek to 'The Stars As They Were', 'Jerry Victory', 'His Parlours Zoo' and a topical budget newsreel running Monday to Wednesday;

and 'A Slate At Sea', 'One Round O'Brien' and a topical budget from Thursday to Saturday.

The report in the *Kettering Leader* dated 7th May stated:

Opening of the Empire
The Empire looks good to begin with and has started life well. A wide gracefully proportioned archway of artistically formed stonework and decoration renders it very pleasing indeed. The interior of the theatre is notably appointed and seated throughout with tip up seats numbering between five and six hundred it is artistically decorated as well as being warmed and aired by methods up-to-date.

Among the features of note is the diffusing light of the main electric lamps and the quaint looking lamps reminiscent of designs more in vogue with ones of a century ago attached to the walls. In the matter of technical equipment the Empire has the last word in projectors by means of which the pictures are displayed in a most perfect manner. With the latest and best films showing there is no need to wonder at the sure success which is attending Kettering's new picture house.

The balcony was small and in later years was to become perhaps the most popular of any cinema in town. It had double seats, described as 'hugging hutches', and were filled nightly with patrons to whom the films showing were only secondary.

The success of the Empire was almost certainly a reason for the demise of the Hippodrome. It had a bijou orchestra regularly playing for the films and providing the interludes. The ensemble comprised of piano and violin for the lesser films, and for the prestige films they were augmented with a bass, cornet and cello. Hardly a grand orchestra, but nevertheless a very competent combination by all accounts, though quite where they were accommodated in the smallish auditorium one can only guess. The prices of admission at this time were Stalls 5d., 9d., and one shilling. The balcony seats were 1/3d. An additional price of 3d. was added later.

Though quite late with the transition to talkies, it was ahead of the Coliseum. The last silent show was Monday, 4th May, 1931 for three days, starring Constance Talmadge in 'Venus of Venice' (1927). It would seem as though the Empire had continued to show silent films until the bitter end, and then fallen back on past films as this film was four years old by then. The proprietor, presumably Bamforth, stated that he was giving up silent films because it was no longer possible to get them, at least up to the Empire standard. The lack of silent films was forcing the change. That seemed to be some sort of apology. The real reason is likely that the Empire was suffering poor attendances, as both the Pavilion and the Victoria Picture House were on 'talkies'. The cinema closed on Thursday, May 7th for the installation of sound and a small refurbishment.

Talkies opened at the Empire on Monday, 11th May, with 'Let Us Be Gay' (1930), starring Norma Shearer. The lateness of the conversion meant that the Empire had the latest projection equipment available at the time.

The demolition begins
(Photo: Evening Telegraph (ET))

Early in 1937, the Empire was taken over by Jack Sherwood, who already owned the New Coliseum. The Empire had become a primarily second-run cinema and therefore could book virtually any film that had already shown in the town's circuit houses. It was a sensible acquisition for Sherwood, as he was able to be on films when the New Coliseum was presenting stage, and of course after the latter theatre's fire.

It was inevitable that it also found audiences for the 'B' pictures and would often run programmes of double feature pictures, with such stars as Hopalong Cassidy and Tex Ritter; the programmes were almost always 'all action pot boilers'. I remember going to see 'San Francisco' (1936), starring Clark Gable and Spencer Tracy, and I think that was likely my first visit to a real cinema. I seem to remember my father booking the tickets at Glovers, the cycle shop on the corner of Montague Street and Eskdail Street. I was, I remember, awestruck by the earthquake scenes.

There must have been other refurbishments, because as a lad I remember it had maroon walls and the ceiling was a pleated fabric material. The proscenium was of Grecian design and the screen tabs were maroon. The most notable feature of the Empire were the 'hugging hutches' – twin seats which were on the back wall of the balcony and where you took your girlfriend to get better acquainted, not necessarily to see the film. I wonder how many wedding bells the Empire was responsible for. It was warm, comfortable and dark, and all for a few shillings; half that, if you went 'Dutch'.

After the Second World War, the Empire's fortunes began to change, unhappily for the worst. It changed hands again, this time to Mr. Joseph Lee. In 1950, Mr. H.D. Pascoe of Northampton took over the cinema and leased it in 1953 to Mr. W.H. Allcock, who had previously run cinemas in Birmingham and Wolverhanpton. A complete redecoration, with more up-to-date projection equipment installed, the cinema received a new name, **NEW EMPIRE**. In little more than a year the cinema closed.

The projection staff in these years were Mr. Bernard Ridley and Mr. P. Cowan, who was the chief projectionist in the Empire's latter years. In the post-war years, when the manager was Mr. Joseph Lee, on the staff was a certain Mr. Emanuel Goldy, who had appeared in a different guise earlier in another Kettering cinema.

Shows were usually continuous from 5.30pm until around 10.45pm. There were also matinees on Thursdays – early closing day in the town – and Saturdays, both at 2.30pm, and running continuous until the end of the day. Sunday performances in later times started at 7pm.

The final shows commenced the week of 13th June, 1954, and were Sunday to Wednesday 'Four Steps In the Clouds' (1942), an Italian film with Gino Servi, supported by 'The Chequered Coat' (1948), starring Tom Conway. Thursday to Saturday the Empire went out in grand style with 'Santa Fe' (1951), starring Randoph Scott, and 'Captive Girl' (1953), starring Johnny Weismuller. A rip-roaring finale to the Empire's life. At 10.30 that evening, THE END flashed on the New Empire screen for the very last time, and the final episode in the Empire story was complete.

The Empire had been a popular house. It was not pretentious and showed the sort of programmes that always had an audience. The last few days were typical of its film fare, so what went wrong?

When William Allcock took over the Empire in 1953, he also had three other cinemas that were very successful, and there was every reason to believe that the Empire would be, too. He was no stranger to the cinema business. At the age of 16 he was one of the first operators to travel to remote parts of the country which had no established cinema. His touring company included a substantial orchestra, whose conductor was Paul Beard, father of the famous orchestra leader of the same name. His claim to fame was that he had toured 'Birth of A Nation' and 'Intolerance', and had shown those films over 2000 times.

With the New Empire, he took over a difficult task. The circuit houses in the town took all of the first run business. To compete he chose to show the better Continental films, alongside the more traditional Empire programmes.

For the first three days of 'Behind Closed Doors' (1953), a French film, we were packed out... then they never came again to see any more excellent foreign films, Allcock explained on closure. I have done everything to save the Eskdail Street house. I booked the right films and had a fair run of the best Continentals. I don't know what the trouble was. This is a family hall and we made a specialty of giving patrons special attention but it seems they are inclined to go out of town for their entertainment. My other cinemas are successful, but in order to compete with the three circuit cinemas in town I had to give the public something different.

One might see that this was the start of the cinema closures in Kettering. Only one cinema had closed previously, and that was the Hippodrome thirty-four years earlier. Over the years the Empire had been quite unfairly called a flea pit. It was never such, nor had been. The Empire did not die because of property deals, unwarranted branding, or boardroom decisions. It died simply because the public left it to do so. Had they continued to support this little cinema, it could well have managed to survive and have preserved the potential for a community cinema framework, and today could have been a nice luxurious hall providing an optional cinema to the mighty multiplex. Instead, nothing now remains except the shell to link it to its past – not even its name up there on the parapet for all to see.

We are thankful for what remains of the old Empire – 1997
(Photo: M. Thornton)

Projection and Technical Information

When the Empire opened in 1920, it had two BECKs and this remained so until the installation of sound. In 1931 the BECKS were replaced with two KALEE 7 projectors with BRITISH ACOUSTIC soundheads and amplification. In 1937 the sound equipment was replaced with DUROSONIC sound. It is likely the projectors were also replaced by KALEE 8s. New speakers were also installed, consisting of treble horn and bass chamber. The treble horn was, in fact, a series of smaller horns, each perfectly matched and arranged in such a way that the sound was 'sprayed' over the auditorium.

In the final refurbishment, the two KALEE 8s were replaced by KALEE 21s. It is thought that a new screen capable of wide screen was installed in 1953, but certainly not CinemaScope, as this only reached Kettering in 1954. There is reference to the BECK projectors obtaining their power from a battery source, but when sound was installed the generative source must have been from the mains. With battery operation, recharging would have been necessary, and it is thought this was done using a gas engine.

Typical Empire film fare
(Photo: Evening Telegraph (ET))

Regal

The owners of this new cinema have a reputation of owning some of the finest cinemas in the country. The Regal Kettering is the finest of them all.

So said the publicity issued prior to the opening of the new super-cinema, which was under construction in the High Street in 1936. For once, publicity was no exaggeration. Super cinemas were in vogue; large picture palaces to match the importance of showing films to the masses in the style and grandeur of the movies themselves. Modern architecture and luxury provided the likes never before enjoyed by the working classes. Temples dedicated to the motion-picture erected in cities and towns. As a fine example of 1930's design and architecture, the Regal, Kettering was no exception. Today its façade is listed.

High Street before 1936
(Photo: Evening Telegraph (ET))

It is difficult to imagine what the impact of this huge building was making on the High Street in those days. Construction started in December 1935 on the site of Messrs. Goosey and Sons, a drapers and fancy goods store of some note. It is not known how the site was acquired but it was of considerable size in width, and ran as far back as to require another site to be cleared in Gas Street (Meadow Road). The design was by George Coles, of London, and the builders were Henry Kent, also of London. The owners, Cohen and Rafler, owned other cinemas both in London and the provinces, one being the Ritz at Southend. The cost was £70,000.

I remember distinctly a large board fronting the scaffolding, which proclaimed the building of a large new super cinema. I was only seven at the time but it stays in the mind. It was certainly the beginnings of an affection which resulted in me working in that building years later, and which today provides me with many happy and treasured memories. It was built within twelve months.

Goosey & Sons drapery store
(Photo: Evening Telegraph (ET))

The façade of the Regal was quite unusual in design and said to be the only one of its style in Europe. The front was dominated by the tower, rising high above the street and topped with a giant halo which, when lit with neon, could be seen for many miles around. Sweeping away from the tower were flanking walls linking the massive buttresses each side, forming the bulk of the frontage. The impressive tower had a thick, glazed glass, brick window formed in three sections, which was illuminated at night from inside with strips of neon changing continuously.

The whole façade was also outlined by neon. The large canopy provided a letterbox for advertising the current films and on the top of the canopy, in single letters, the word REGAL was also outlined in neon. Though the neon display was to be darkened later, it was a wonderful sight, and I remember all those years ago watching the lights changing. It was the focal point of the High Street.

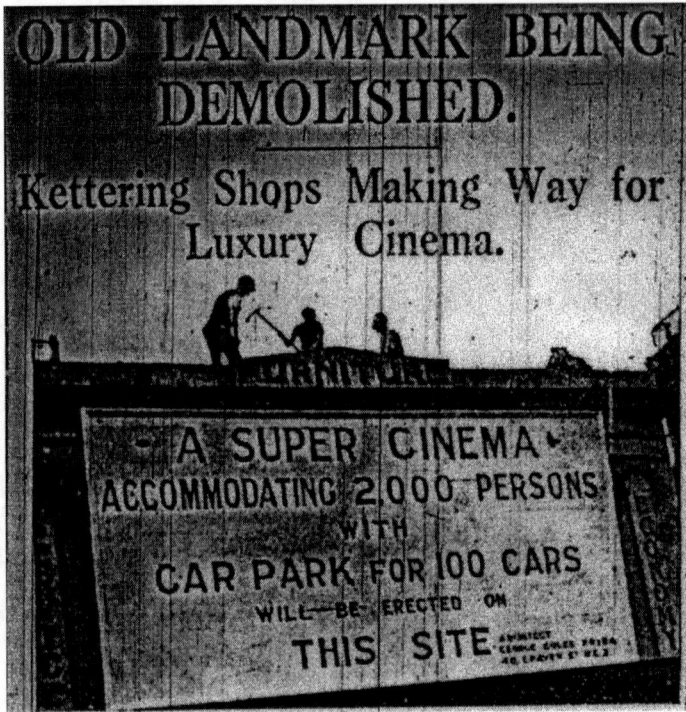

Hoarding for the construction of the new super cinema and demolition begins (Photo: Evening Telegraph (ET))

Inside, the cinema was even more impressive. Five pairs of entrance doors led into a large foyer. There were pay desks each side, one for the stalls and one for the circle and a large sales area. Another set of doors led into the magnificent vestibule.

The vestibule was lavishly furnished with two large luxury couches back-to-back in the centre. Lighting was by a large central feature and smaller wall lights. The ceiling was designed with sunken panels in art deco-style. Either side, two huge plated mirrors gave a spacious ambience. The area was lavished with potted palms and exotic plants.

The vestibule was used for advertising forthcoming films and regularly staged exhibitions related to specific events. During WW2 there was a full-sized cockpit of a Spitfire advertising Wings For Victory Week and another of a mock-up of a warship bridge for Warship Week, when funds were raised for Kettering's own warship H.M.S. *Pytchley*. Overall, the vestibule gave an air of elegance and opulence.

Either side of the steps down to the stalls were two large supporting pillars, which were hollow at first floor level. Each side of these were stairs leading to the terrace café and circle. The hollow pillars served a useful purpose; one being the restaurant office, and the other a telephone kiosk. At the far end of the café were two sets of doors. One set led to the circle and toilets, and the other was an exit passage from the rear of the circle and the way to the projection room.

View of the High Street after construction of the Regal
(Photo: D. Wharton)

89

Before entering the circle, there was a circular vestibule which accommodated the washrooms. Steps led from this vestibule up into the centre of the circle. The best seats ran down to the front and the less expensive ran to the rear. There was little difference to the quality, and all had excellent sight lines.

The auditorium was very modern and 1930s art deco. The ceiling was a series of 'stepped' levels down to the wide arched proscenium. Concealed lighting panels ran the length of the ceiling, styled in the cinema's corporate opal glass and scrolled metalwork. In the stalls, the underside of the large circle was decorated with three large roundels which served as air conditioning ducts. While the vestibule was in pink, the auditorium was decorated in shades of buff. The proscenium was modern plasterwork designed with a fluted pattern. Behind this was three-colour lighting, which changed constantly.

There was an orchestra pit, but no under-stage access. Small display areas were set each side of the stage and contained similar foliage found in the vestibule. The stage was quite large, with an apron front. The screen was on the back wall. Behind that was the speaker chamber, which was accessed from the car park. The stage had three sets of tabs (curtains). Those which covered the screen were silver and fluted. The front tabs were golden. The third was a little in front of the screen tabs and was of a type so unique that only a few were ever installed. A festoon, or contour curtain, it could be set to 59 different patterns either manually or automatically. When programmed, the curtain could go through a complete cycle in five minutes.

There were four dressing rooms and staff rooms. Air conditioning was achieved by using a new 'air washing' system, keeping the interior of the cinema always fresh with clean air. The stage was over fifty feet wide and thirty feet deep.

In later years when I worked at the cinema, I would often stand on the stage and look into the auditorium. The view was awesome, showing the real size and magnificence. One could easily understand why bands and artistes loved to play the Regal.

To appreciate the importance of the new cinema, I reproduce a press report from the *Kettering Leader* dated 11th December 1936.

Spacious vestibule of the Regal (Photo: J. Winfield)

The Circle (Photo: J. Winfield)

The Stalls area. Note the festoon curtain set in one of its 59 sequences
(Photo: J. Winfield)

A regal staff photograph taken in 1946. Centre of the second row is Jack Goldy
and far left is Emanuel Goldy, Eric Walters, chief projectionist is fourth from
right also in the second row.

Modern Cinema Marvels

With the nearing completion of the Regal cinema at Kettering the term 'modern cinema marvels' could be an appropriate description of the new Kettering super-cinema which is to be opened shortly. Up-to-date, magnificent and modern in every way it is a veritable hall of wonders. As a luxury cinema it is one of the finest in the provinces and money has not been spared in its fitting out. The best of everything has been initiated to make the Regal in many ways a unique theatre with its own particular niche in cinema history. The unusual front with its tall and dignified tower, flanked each side with massive buttresses, has completely altered the appearance of the High Street. Its construction has been watched with great interest. The tower will be illuminated with the newest neon lighting equipment which will change through pale blue down to pale pink. Inside the tower, hidden away from view behind thick glass are perpendicular neon strips which are illuminated alternately in the different colours to give this effect.

The interior of the cinema has the air circulated with modern equipment. The air is drawn into the cinema first passing through this equipment where it is washed and purified before being circulated through the building. For showing the films the finest equipment has been obtained and installed. The arc lamps have been brought into Britain especially and the latest devices for the protection of the patrons installed.

The Regal opened on Boxing Day, December 26th, 1936, amid tremendous razzle-dazzle. The opening programme was fully attended and every one of the near 2000 seats, grey in the stalls and 'fitted' blue in the circle, was filled.

The opening was broadcast on Radio Normandie, which was apparently a pre-opening 'commercial' and the first time such a method was used for this purpose. Little detail exists but reports suggest that the broadcast comprised the story of the new cinema, its opening, and a snippet from the soundtrack of 'Everything Is Rhythm'.

Although no celebrity from the film world attended, there were crowds in the High Street taking in the atmosphere of the prestigious event. The

Regal shone like the glittering jewel that it was, its neon lighting up the street in shades of blue, green, yellow and red, and with merged colours and outlining the corners and outlines of the building. The mushroomed top on the tower, lit with a blue neon, took on the resemblance of a giant halo. It was the best Christmas decoration the town had ever witnessed and it would be there night after night. A review of the opening by a reporter, read as follows:

REGAL
SUPER CINEMA
PHONE 3232
CAR PARK **KETTERING** CAFE

GRAND OPENING CEREMONY
By THE RIGHT HONOURABLE EARL SPENSER DL

BOXING DAY   SATURDAY DECEMBER 26TH, 1936   at 8pm

PRELUDE AND OVERTURE by
MUNN AND FELTONS WORKS BAND

FANFARE

THE HERALD TRUMPETERS

OPENING ADDRESS AND CEREMONY BY THE R.H. EARL SPENSER DL
and THE CHAIRMAN OF KETTERING URBAN DISTRICY COUNCIL
Followed by an address by Mr. Morley-Clarke, Manager of the Regal

•

On The Screen

IVOR MORETON and DAVE KAYE with HARRY ROY and his BAND in
EVERYTHING IS RHYTHM (u)
ALSO
**BUILDING A BUILDING
AUDIOSCOPIX in 3-D**

On The Stage

PETROLINGRO and his LADIES HUSSAR Broadcasting Band

•

For the REGAL's BIG BROADCAST tune to RADIO NORMANDIE at 2.30pm on
Christmas Day

Programme for the Regal opening ceremony

The Regal Kettering, the town's new 2000-seater super-cinema, was declared open on Boxing Day before a full audience. Built on the most modern lines the Regal has a striking façade reputed to be the only one of its kind in Europe. Besides providing first class entertainment it plays a large part in brightening the main street of the town. Munn and Feltons Works Band filled the orchestra pit providing an enjoyable musical programme before the opening ceremony. Four trumpeters heralded the opening ceremony and then Mr. Morely-Clark, the General Manager, welcomed the audience from the stage *saying that although Kettering had five cinemas now he pledged that the Regal would be able to offer a wider variety of entertainment which would include stage as well as screen. Then followed a film 'Building A Building' which told the story of the building of the Regal from its commencement to completion and it sparkled with the humour provided by the workers involved. Spectacles with red and green eyepieces, issued to all patrons on entering, were donned to see 'Audioscopics'** a hilarious little picture filmed in the third dimension. The official opening then took place by the R.H. Earl Spencer followed by an address by the Chairman of the Council. Finally there followed the entertaining film 'Everything Is Rhythm' starring Harry Roy and his Band. The evening came to an end with a delightful concert by Petrolingo and his Ladies Hussar Band.*

* Audioscopics was an MGM Pete Smith Speciality short, filmed in the anaglyph 3-D process.

That programme ran for the whole of the following week. Getting down to the business of drawing the crowds, top films were lined up, starting with the first showing in Kettering of Gracie Fields in 'Queen of Hearts'. Sunday evening celebrity concerts were staged, which became the hallmark of excellent entertainment and had people travelling in from all parts of the county. Top broadcasting bands of the day topped the bill, including Ambrose, Joe Loss, Jack Hylton, Henry Hall and many others. Top recording and radio artists made regular appearances, as did Rawicz and Landaur, Anne Zeigler and Webster Booth, and film stars George Formby and Arthur Askey. It is said that Reginald Foorte played at the Regal; this is not substantiated, although he could have played an electronic organ.

The beloved Flanagan and Allan appeared at the cinema, as did Vera Lynn with Ambrose. These celebrity concerts continued throughout the years of WW2 but were soon interspersed with the 'hostilities only' Sunday film performances, granted due to the 'garrison' increase in the town's population.

Some of the greatest films of the 1940s played at the Regal, including the Kettering showing of 'Gone With The Wind', which played for two weeks – quite unusual for a provincial cinema – only to return for another engagement a few weeks later. Queues stretched along the High Street and well down Gas Street (Meadow Road). I can remember going with my parents to see this phenomenal film, though quite what I understood of it then I am not sure. But I did see it first time around.

Publicity for a regular Sunday celebrity concert the Regal was renowned for (Photo: Evening Telegraph (ET))

I saw so many of the great films of the 1930s and 40s at the Regal. It was my 'palace'; I would visit all of Kettering's cinemas, but the Regal was my favourite. I often dreamed of a visit to the projection room, but little did I know that one day I would work there.

Seat prices were modest for this super cinema. Front stalls 6d., Centre Stalls 9d., Rear Stalls 1/-, Rear Circle was 1/6d, and Front Circle 2/-. For the Sunday concerts the prices were 6d., 1/-, and 1/6d for the Stalls, though reversed the dearest at the front and for the Circle 2/- and 2/6d. By 1946 prices had risen but were still very reasonable for a cinema of this calibre, with the stalls at 10d., 1/- and 1/9d., and the circle at 2/3d. and 2/9d.

After hostilities finished, there were moves by the Essoldo chain to acquire the Regal, but this fell through. Towards the end of 1947 negotiations took place between the owners and Granada Theatres Ltd, a London-based cinema circuit who had cinemas in the Home Counties, the nearest one being at Bedford.

At the end of hostilities the splendid neon display was restored, after being blacked out for six years, but the ravages of weather and lack of maintenance had reduced its effect. Alas it was never returned to its former spectacle and thus a part of the old Regal glory had disappeared forever.

The last show at the REGAL was a double-bill, 'Quiet Wedding' (1940), starring Margaret Lockwood and Derek Farr, and 'Broadway' (1942), with George Raft.

Two interesting mysteries remain. In the original plans there was to be a Wurlitzer Organ installed, but it never happened; and why was the originally proposed name SAVOY changed to REGAL? The Savoy in Russell Street had not been built at that time, so there was no clash of names. The questions may never be answered but one thing is for sure, naming the cinema as Regal was an apt name for it was the grandest cinema in the county. Truly a 'people's palace'.

Projection and Technical Information

The Regal was originally fitted out with ROSS FC1 projectors. The sound system was RCA with, it is thought, Photophone soundheads as was the amplification. The Arc Lamps were ROSS high intensity. There was a Premier Slide projector and a Strand Sun follow spot. The projection room was spacious and airy with a lantern roof, suitably shaded. A twin non-sync unit occupied one end of the room and at the other was the Strand three-colour stage lighting board. The stage had front and screen tabs and there was the splendid festoon drop curtain mid-stage, which could be controlled from either the stage or the projection room.

Sometime in the following years the ROSS FC1s were replaced with ROSS GC3s, but it is likely it was done with the acquisition by Granada Theatres. The screen was standard Academy ratio and on the back wall of the stage. The speaker assembly was housed in a sound chamber built onto the rear wall of the cinema. The cinema had an air-conditioning system plant which has been described earlier.

Granada

Granada stands as the word for a guarantee of intimate comfort, good programming and 'Service with a Smile'.

The grand facade of the Regal now in Granada hands (Photo: Photo Coverage)

This was the pledge made by the new manager, Mr. W. Bush, when he arrived at the Regal cinema in the first week of 1948. The process of 'Granada-ising' was begun. It was not such a difficult task, as the patrons of the Regal had enjoyed a similar policy of service for many years, but the cinema had become jaded with the austerity of the war years. The real task was to actually make the changeover, as names and old friends die hard. For Mr. Bush, it was not made easier by there being no break for redecoration, or even a short break at changeover. The show went on and there was no refurbishment apart from the change of name and some cosmetic work front of house.

The main drive for change came with the advertisements in the local paper which simply, but effectively, said REGAL begin saying GRAH-NAH-DAH. This was re-enforced by the removal of the Regal sign from the canopy, and a large fin erected on the buttress adjoining the bank which carried GRANADA in the company's corporate style.

From the first day, the staff members were turned out in their new uniforms. Blue suits and peak caps for the male floor staff. For the girls it was a dark blue skirt, gold satin blouse and a chic hat. To add to this, they also wore a blue cape with gold lining. They looked stunning. New internal displays and signage enhanced the new image. On the screen, the Granada-style day-sets and logos appeared, with the circuit's corporate style of film presentation the order of the day.

Granada Theatres were owned and run by the Bernstein family. It was a relatively small circuit until after WW2, at which time it began buying up cinemas beyond its traditional boundaries of London and the South, though it did have some cinemas in other parts of the country. Both Sidney and Cecil were fully active in the business and ran the cinemas to a very high standard. The flagship was the Granada at Tooting, an elaborate and beautiful 'cinema palace' held as the benchmark for all eighty or so Granada circuit cinemas, regardless of their individual name. The Kettering Granada would benefit for many years as part of the circuit.

The impressive vestibule, entrance to the circle and restaurant. Note the electrolier which was corporate for all Granada theatres
(Photo: Photo Coverage)

*Granada auditorium. Picture taken after the CinemaScope installation in 1954.
The speakers on the proscenium and the one flown were installed for the 'pop
package' shows (Photo: J. Winfield)*

The first programme to show at the Granada was on Monday,
4th January, 1948, being 'Squadron Leader X' (1942), starring Eric
Portman and Ann Dvorak. For the first few weeks, according to press
advertisements, second-run films were programmed but eventually first-
run films from Associated British-Pathe, MGM and Warner Bros were
exhibited, as well as films from independent studios.

The stage presentations seemed to fall off for a while, though there
were programmes of Cine-variety, which Granada were well known for
presenting. Concerts were regularly held involving local artistes, and
Sunday night variety slots by local aspiring performers.

At the beginning of the 1950s the Granada got its long-awaited
refurbishment. It was accomplished without closure. For weeks audiences
would see tall scaffolding within the auditorium and elsewhere, the work
being accomplished through the night and right up to minutes before the
day performances began. The colour schemes were bold and exciting

reds, blues, blacks, gold, greens and other shades.

The interior lighting totally changed, with a large electrolier – found in all major Granadas – suspended above the stalls, with smaller ones above and under the circle and repeated in the foyers. Constructed in gilded metal work and opal tinted glass, they had to be 'dropped' periodically for cleaning and maintenance. How I remember that operation, having to climb up into the void above the auditorium and winding down the massive light. I was always mindful of the 1942 film, 'Phantom of the Opera' and fancied myself as a 'Claud Raines' let loose with a hacksaw. It was a morning's job for all of the projection staff. How many 60 watt bulbs (or were they 100watt?) it used, I fail to remember, but they all had to be changed. Removed 'good' ones were used elsewhere. Nothing was wasted by Granada.

The proscenium was remodelled with a new design and finished in mottled blue-grey and gilt surround. I always felt that this was a mistake, as the old Regal proscenium was very attractive and aesthetic. The remainder of the interior of the cinema was decorated in the bold colours the Granada Group seemed to like. It certainly did give a luxurious look and feel to the cinema.

The two pay desks were reduced to one. A snack bar was created in the front foyer. The two settees in the vestibule were long gone, but the potted palms and full mirror remained. There was an atmosphere of modernity and good fortune as one passed through to climb the stairs to the circle or descend to the stalls.

Many prestige films played at the Granada. In 1953 3-Dimension was successfully presented, and many of the films made in that format were shown, including the very first 'Bwana Devil' (1952) and the very last film made in Natural Vision 3-D 'Kiss Me Kate' (1953), probably the last provincial cinema to do so. Natural Vision 3-D was quite different to the Anaglyph system used when 3-D was shown at the Regal all those years ago. While spectacles were still required to be worn to produce 3-D, they resembled sunglasses and the image was in colour. A special projection synchronising unit toured the Granada theatres chosen to show the format, which also included a stereophonic sound integrator which provided the ambient sound.

IT'S THE WONDER OF

4 TRACK MAGNETIC STEREOPHONIC SOUND

THAT GIVES REALISM TO THE MIRACLE OF

CINEMASCOPE

Standard film has a single optical sound track; all the sounds come from one point only.

BUT the vast panorama of Cinemascope demands life-like reproduction of voices, of music, of all sounds. Stereophonic sound achieves this by the use of **4 MAGNETIC SOUND TRACKS** on the film.

These **4 MAGNETIC SOUND TRACKS** through 24 speakers, scientifically placed, ensure that every whisper, every word, every musical note and every sound comes to you from the direction in which it would actually come in real life . . . and with a clarity and perfection of tone that has never before been achieved in any medium.

AT LAST . . .
REALISTIC SOUND
ONLY BY
4 TRACK
MAGNETIC
STEREOPHONIC
SOUND
AND . . . ONLY AT **GRANADA**
KETTERING OCT. 1954

GRANADAGRAM NUMBER 159

We've spent much time composing a rhyme
on something most spectacular,

Only to find it's a bit of a bind
to put it in the vernacular.

It's easy enough to write some stuff
with 'moon' and 'June' around,

But how on earth can a poet give birth
to a sonnet on **GRANADA**'s
wonderful installation of
4-TRACK MAGNETIC
STEREOPHONIC
KETTERING 1954   SOUND

Advanced publicity and a 'GranadaGram' for the coming of CinemaScope in 1954 (Photo: Granada theatres)

With the advent of CinemaScope, the Granada was the first to install it in the county – and with full stereophonic sound to boot. Most MGM and Warner Bros. films were presented, including the popular musicals. The Granada presented the first CinemaScope release, 'The Robe', in October 1954. There were queues around the block, with four shows on Saturday. Nothing had been seen like this since 'Gone With The Wind' and would not again until the cinema played 'Sound of Music'.

This innovation came from 20th Century-Fox. An 'anamorphic' system which squeezed the image horizontally during filming and un-squeezed it during projection, giving a visual image on the screen two-and-a-half times the width to height, with the added magnetic soundtracks. Independent houses were wooed by Fox, as the Rank organisation would only install it in prestigious cinemas. The result? The Granada was running the latest releases which the Odeon and Gaumont could not.

Hugely popular at the Granada were the pop-package one night stands which were staged from 1958. Just about every British, and many American, pop star of the day appeared on the stage with a twice nightly show. It was wild and very noisy but the Kettering 'fans' loved it all. At 5/-, 7/- and front stalls at 10/- (you paid the most to be deafened the most), the shows were staged every few weeks and fanatically received.

Fortunes were to wane, however. In 1968 the Granadiers Saturday morning Children's Club closed. In February 1974 the stalls were closed up and seating confined to the circle only. It came as a big shock when in June of the same year, Granada Theatres announced that the cinema would close. Saturday, June 8th, saw the final performances, ending a seven day run of 'Zardoz', starring Sean Connery and Charlotte Rampling. It was an inglorious end, as the film was slated as being a *glittering cultural trash pile.*

Stalwarts could hardly have left the Granada that night with anything less than dejection. At the end of the last performance 'So Long, Farewell' – lifted from the 'Sound of Music' – was played. A pity that film was not shown as the last performance. At least it would have drawn a goodly crowd and been a fitting finale to the life of a 'modern cinema miracle'. A few weeks later, the Granada was on Bingo.

In 1952, I was to achieve my boyhood ambition to get into that projection room. I began work with Granada Theatres and was assigned to work at the cinema which had been so much a feature of my childhood. Living away at the time, I could not but feel great sorrow when hearing that the Granada had closed as a cinema. My associations with the cinema had reached back to its very beginnings, and I felt a sense of losing what had been a part of my life.

Granada staff photograph

Projection and Technical Information

Ross GC3s were the projectors for much of the Granada days. These versatile machines were adaptable to the new developments in film projection, particularly 3-Dimension and CinemaScope. For Polaroid Natural-Vision 3-D, which required both projectors operating the left and right-hand prints, a 'portable' Selsyn synchronisation unit was imported and installed between the projectors. Special lenses were fitted along with apertures, and polarization filters were placed before the projection lenses. A special Mirrorglo screen was installed, replacing the Academy ratio screen. An imported stereophonic sound unit was also installed, particularly for Warnerphonic sound which accompanied the Warner Bros 3-D productions.

For CinemaScope 4000ft. spool boxes were fitted to the Ross FCs. The Stereophonic 4-track magnetic soundheads were fitted immediately below the upper spool box, the sound reproduction being in retard of the appropriate film frame. Sound amplification required four amplifier racks. The Anamorphic lenses for each projector were Kalee Variamorphs.

The sound system throughout was RCA. The magnetic soundheads were model RCA LM9010. These were self-drive, by which the film was drawn over a stabilizing drum and then across a four-track magnetic cluster. The normal optical soundhead remained. For the stereophonic sound, four pre-amplifiers were used to boost the magnetic signals to levels comparable to optical sound. From the pre-amps the signals were passed to three standard voltage amplifiers. A fourth amplifier supplied the 'effects' track signal through a suppressor (to ensure evenly diffused sound) to the 24 ambient speakers around the auditorium. Changeover to/from magnetic or optical was by a photo-magnetic switch.

The screen was 52ft wide by 20ft high. It was mounted on a tubular frame and set well back allowing room for stage presentations.

Later, the date not recorded, the Ross GCs were replaced by PHILIPS FP7 projectors and WESTREX sound. For stage shows, special imported amplification was installed.

No longer a cinema, but still with us (Photo: M. Thornton)

Odeon 8-Screen Multiplex
The magic lives on

Nestled in the corner of the Kettering Retail Park, by the A14 road, is Pegasus Court. An apt name perhaps, because it is here that can be found the latest example of a temple for the showing of motion-pictures… the ODEON; an eight-screen modern multiplex providing the choice of the latest films in a state-of -the art environment; and what's more, returning a familiar and welcome cinema name to the town.

The ODEON is a pleasant and well-designed building that manages to retain that special luxury feeling of a super cinema of the past. It was in 1995 that the first rumblings were heard of the building of a multiplex in Kettering, and there was a threat of the town becoming a cinematic wilderness. Because of lack of support for the two-screened OHIO, the latest films could not be booked, and it appears that movie-goers preferred to travel to either Northampton or Milton Keynes. Only a few supporters, and those lacking mobility, visited the OHIO; the mobile young completely shunned the twin screens.

In 1996 it was announced that a site for the new cinema had finally been chosen and building would begin, however there was some delay and the construction fell behind schedule.

The cinema is built on a site which also has restaurants, pub amenities and shopping services, as well as ample car parking. Near to the edge of town, it is close to large residential estates and an urbanised area, and has good access to public transport; the potential usage is enormous. The developers, Farrho Developments, completed the work in December 1997.

The clean lines of a modern cinema concept
(Photo: M. Thornton)

The **ODEON** opened with an extravaganza on the 11th December, with the full 8-screen programme opening the following day.

The opening featured a premiere preview of the current James Bond 007 thriller, 'Tomorrow Never Dies'. To add to the occasion, supermodel of the age, Caprice, and TV star Dani Behr made personal appearances, supported by local musicians and artistes. An Aston Martin DB5, owned by Chris Brigstock, was on display on the forecourt. It had been featured in the film and in an earlier Bond feature, 'Goldeneye' (1996). Alongside the Aston Martin stood the BMW motor cruiser, also featured in the film. The opening ceremony was a spectacular event.

The first full programme of screenings started briskly the next morning and consisted of nine films spread over the eight screens:

****

THE BORROWERS (1997) starring John Goodman
THE FULL MONTY (1997) starring Robert Carlyle
BOND-TOMORROW NEVER DIES (1997) starring Pierce Brosnan
HERCULES (1997) Disney Animation
G.I.JANE (1997) starring Demi Moore
FACE/OFF (1997) starring John Travolta, Nicholas Cage
I KNOW WHAT YOU DID LAST SUMMER (1997) Jennifer Love Hewitt
COPLAND (1997) starring Sylvester Stallone
ALIEN-RESURECTION (1997) starring Sigourney Weaver
****

Kettering had never witnessed such a choice of films since the days with five cinemas in town. The films were shown at convenient times for patronage, and presented in the various screens to accommodate the demand. The new cinema, although out of the centre of town, was an immediate success and the movie-starved punters flocked to the cinemas. It is recorded as having been one of Odcon's best performing multiplexes at the time.

The exterior of the ODEON is impressive and a welcome change from the bland architecture of multiplex buildings in general. It looks like a cinema and less like a furniture warehouse, and its two tall buttresses immediately take the eye. They support the abutment and modern canopy, which is illuminated. ODEON is massively displayed in silver across this abutment. The buttresses are of a cubic design and faced in a greyish-blue tile.

The main part of the building is pentagonal in shape. The entrance is of three sets of glass doors with panoramic glass panels, above which 8-SCREEN CINEMA is displayed. The whole building is modern stone masonry and brick, golden in colour with a grey/blue pattern running horizontally around the outside of the building. At night the complex is illuminated with red and blue neon and the buttresses are floodlit in blue.

Once inside, the ambience is one of luxury and spaciousness. The foyer is adorned with neon and decorative lighting. Sales points offer soft drinks and beverages, the ever-popular popcorn, and a range of fast foods. The ticket desk is available either for the daily performances or for advanced bookings, and a 'queue-busting' system is available for patrons using card payments. The décor is of tasteful shades of blue and grey, the ODEON's corporate colours with added blacks and whites. The carpets are similarly patterned.

A decorative feature of the foyer is the ceiling. Curved metal designs support the illumination. Above is a large circular dome, across which is displayed the ODEON logo by the use of a Kinetic projector. This is further enhanced by red and blue neon. The result is a very attractive and pleasing décor.

The vestibule and concessions area (Photo: M. Thornton)

A designated carpet 'footpath' leads to the eight screens which comprise the multiplex. Each screen is stadium-seated and the walls are dark textured and light grey panelling. Seats are moquette-styled, in the corporate colours, with excellent leg room and comfortably postured. Seating for the disabled is available in all screens. The floors are deep carpeted in grey.

Each screen has a set of grey tabs. Lighting is provided by spotlights displayed on the wall panels and is selective. The seating capacities are: Screen 1, 175 seats; Screen 2, 125 seats; Screen 3, 232 seats; Screen 4, 349 seats; Screen 5, 105 seats; Screen 6, 83 seats; Screen 7, 105 seats; Screen 8, 310 seats. In the larger screens the ODEON logo is projected across the screen tabs, as in the foyer. This is pleasantly received and was the first Odeon in the circuit to feature this experimental display. Each auditorium has eight ambient speakers to relay the multi-tracked sound system.

The projection suite is well appointed, spacious and airy. All screens are served by individual projection. Not all screens receive the same sound, however. Screens 1,3, 4 & 8 have full THX Dolby Pro-logic digital sound and the remainder have Dolby Analogue stereo sound.*

The multiplex is attractive, comfortable and an enjoyable environment, making going to the pictures a pleasure. On my visit, the staff were pleasant and helpful. This new cinema was a welcome addition to the town and a fitting way to celebrate one hundred years of cinema in Kettering.

Projection and Technical Information
Projection… 8 x Cinemecannica Victoria 5 projectors (1 for each screen)
Sound Systems… 8 x Cinemecannica CNR 3-35 complete with QSC UIA 900
Amplification (adjacent to each projector)
Screens 1,3,4 & 8 CP 500 Dolby ProLogic THX sound
Screens 2,5,6 &7 C445 Dolby Stereo-surround
Light source… Cinemecannica Zenon
Speakers… High definition and bass resolution – rear screen
8 two-way Audiom ambient speakers… hall

Film feed system… 8 x Cinemecannica auto-feed three platter units
Automation… 8 x Cinemation units (adjacent to each projector)
Special Effects Lighting… Screens 1,3,4 & 8 & Foyer Octo-Kinetic
  projection

*Since 2012 the projection equipment has likely changed from
35mm to digital and the 35mm machines removed, however confirmation
of this had not been received from Odeon at the time of publishing.*

The Odeon at dusk (Photo: M. Thornton)

Part 4

THE OTHER PICTURE SHOWS
CENTRAL HALL
WORKING MEN'S CLUB
THE WICKSTEED PARK

I have spoken only of the commercial cinemas of Kettering. The story does not end there, however, as motion-picture entertainment could be found in many other establishments in the town, particularly in the Working Men's Clubs which have a history nationwide of such provision in their entertainment programmes. The Working Men's Club in Wellington Street had a fully equipped projection room and operated it cinema-style. It may come as a surprise to know that the old Central Hall showed film (although only occasionally) and the Wicksteed Park provided screened entertainment. As this book is a celebration of cinema in Kettering, they have a rightful place within it.

K.I.C.S. Central Hall

When the Victoria Hall converted to a cinema in 1920, there was no public hall in the town. It was felt that there was a need for one but the local council were either reluctant or unable to build one. The Kettering Industrial Co-operative Society (KICS) was an extremely progressive co-operative movement and had a history going back to the 'Rochdale Pioneers'.

They owned a lot of property in the town, particularly around Eden Street and St. Andrews Street. In 1928 the Town Council expressed a wish to have a public hall and the KICS said it was willing to build one, subject to the Society being permitted to hold meetings and the like within it. This agreed, the hall was built by the KICS works department and fitted out as a large public entertainments facility for the town.

Built on a strip of land stretching from Montague Street to Eden Street, it took in existing stables and harness room on which the Long Room – a self-contained facility for small functions and part of the hall – was constructed. The main hall was set back into an arcade which gave access to Newland Street and to the KICS departmental store. To one side of the Montague Street entrance was a chemist shop and on the other a babywear and sundries shop, both owned by the KICS. The entrance to the central hall was by a set of marble steps leading to quite ornate, panelled doors bearing large iron ring handles. Each side were pillars adorned with electric lamps designed as torches. A canopy was erected over the Montague Street entrance to the arcade, which was ornately decorated and had the inscription CENTRAL - K.I.C.S. - HALL.

The Central Hall opened on October 19th, 1929, with the ceremony conducted by the KICS President Thomas Adams, accompanied by the Chairman and Councillors of the Kettering Urban District Council. After the speeches, there followed a celebrity concert given by local artistes, including Carol Summers and Will Eagle.

Entrance to the hall was directly through a small foyer and then double doors. Stairs to the balcony were to each side of the foyer. The floor of the hall was of supreme maple wood, making it a superb floor for dancing and one of the best in the county. To protect the floor when the portable seating was set out, a special canvas was rolled out; when not in use, it was stowed in the Green Room. When set out, the seating consisted of cinema-type plush seats around the perimeter of the hall.

The remainder of the seating was wooden with cushioning, and assembled in sections. When the hall was used for dancing and exhibitions, this seating was man-handled through under-stage doors into the Green Room. The balcony had fixed, plush, cinema-style tip-up seats. The seating capacity was 850 in the main hall and 200 in the balcony. This was reduced to around 600 in the main hall due to fire regulations. The hall had a Minstrel Gallery and a domed ceiling.

Arcade and entrance for the Central Hall in 1929
(Photo: D. Wharton)

The stage was 28ft. wide, quite high, steeply sloped towards the footlights. The front tabs (curtains) were royal blue with gold braid. Forward of them was a safety curtain, on which a pleasant scene was painted. It is not known if this curtain was an 'iron' or fire-proofed canvas. The back cloth was painted with a garden scene and the stage was fully equipped.

Stage productions were regularly presented, especially by the Kettering Operatic Society. There was a projection room which was built out from the rear wall of the building. One can only assume that it was perhaps an afterthought, as it was only accessible by an iron ladder from the roof of the arcade. The Central Hall seemingly was never used for cinema performances, though films were projected there probably as part of lectures and commercial enterprises. The projection room was never fitted out for sound; strange, as in the year of its opening the 'talkies' were being installed in cinemas everywhere.

There are two recorded events that used film presentation. On October 9th, 1931, Amy Johnson, the famous aviator, gave an illustrated lecture about her solo flight to Australia, entitled 'How Jason and I Flew to the Land of the Golden Fleece' (Jason was the name of her Tiger Moth biplane). The *Evening Telegraph* printed a review, part of which is reproduced.

During the showing of the film of the scenes of her welcome in Australia, Amy sat on the raised part of the stage, perfectly at ease, and put her comment, much of it humorous. The film provided a fitting climax to a remarkable lecture.

As an aside, Amy apparently flew to the lecture but was forced to make a forced landing at Grendon the previous evening, because of tiredness.

There was one other advertised film presentation at the Central Hall, which was for the Kettering Radio Show held between September 24th and 26th, 1936, at which national and local radio dealers exhibited. Free film shows were being offered for this event. Whether other shows took place, is open to question.

During WW2, when the hall was given over to billet American service personnel, the projection equipment was removed, never to again be installed. The hall suffered appalling damage during this period, particularly to the panelling and the precious dance floor. This was restored after the hostilities and once again the Central Hall became one of the county's best dance halls; if you wanted to see and be seen, that is where you went on a Saturday night.

Sometime in 1978 the Leicester Co-operative Society took over the KICS, and the Central Hall closed unceremoniously. It became a warehouse and a furniture shop. While the Central Hall was never a cinema in that sense, it had a small contribution to local motion-picture history.

Projection and Technical Information
One Kalee 7 silent projector (maybe two projectors, but not likely).
No sound equipment was ever installed.
A Premier cinema slide lantern.
Screen roll-up installed on stage.

Working Men's Club, Wellington Street

Many cinemas, particularly in coal mining communities, started their lives in Working Men's Clubs. These clubs were a popular and important part of the lives of the working class from around the 1880s onwards, and many still exist today. Not only were they a place where a working man could spend some of his hard-earned leisure time, but a place where he could take his wife and family into an environment more suitable to that of the public houses of the day, and where cheaper drinks and a good social atmosphere could be enjoyed.

Often the clubs also provided libraries, reading rooms, educational services, outings, children's play areas, and a provision of many social and welfare services. One thing they were popular for was their entertainment – concerts, dancing, lunches, etc – so it is not surprising that, in some, motion-pictures were exhibited.

The Kettering Working Men's Club was founded in 1887 and is the part fronting Wellington Street. The Concert Hall was added in 1897 and consisted of a two-storey construction, the lower floor given over to a large billiards room and the upper floor to a bar and concert room. The concert room was separated from the bar area by a large, heavy, wooden partition, which closed off part of the room but opened part-way for the passage of waiters serving drinks. Entrance was either by the main club stairs to the upper floors and then through the new bar, or by a set of rear stairs directly into the concert room.

The concert room was quite large and could seat around five hundred people, with chairs and tables set out intermittently for concerts, and to the sides of the hall for dancing. The stage was quite large with a painted canvas proscenium and dressing rooms off stage each side. The curtains were gold plain material and a painted backdrop. The walls were cream and woodwork oak. Lighting would have been gas originally, but when electricity was installed gas was retained as the secondary lighting.

A projection room was built on the rear end of the concert hall as an addition some years later, probably in the late 1920s, and the entrance to it was off the stairs directly up to the concert room. It is thought that films were probably shown in the latter part of the silent era though no records are forthcoming.

Using the local newspaper as a guide, it seems that the first advertisements for showing films at the 'Works' (as it was popularly known) was for Christmas 1933, and they were 'talkies'. This suggests that sound equipment had been installed by that time. For the morning of Christmas Day and the evening of the day after Boxing Day, talkies were advertised. Christmas Day evening had a concert advertised and Boxing night was dancing.

From then onwards, the Works was screening films every weekend during the summer months, mixed with concerts and dancing during the winter. Films were shown every Sunday lunchtime, which were usually more adult so children were not admitted. These were not 'adult' films as are now categorised, but often horror or gangster films with adult certificates.

Every member of the club could attend, and full members could sign in visitors. Prices for the pictures were usually 3d. and 4d., rising later to 4d. and 6d. Children were half-price and retired pensioner members free. The Saturday shows were always family programmes. In the winter there were comedy and family feature films. In the summer the programme would be of shorts. I can't tell you how many Pathe Gazette musical interludes I saw there; far too many. The Sunday shows were always feature films. This was the first Sunday showing of films in the town.

Sheila Mulligan remembers those shows. She would go to what she called the 'proper cinema' on Saturday morning but remembers the Works, because she could see her favourite films again; but this time clutching her cream soda. She also recollects the lovely evenings of dancing and the concerts.

She recalls the films at the 'Works', although not new, were nevertheless good and if we had already seen them in a 'proper' cinema they were worth seeing over again. In the War the Concert Hall became requisitioned and that was the end of the pictures. The partition doors were locked and bolted. The Concert Room floor was beautiful maple wood and suffered awfully from the army boots but why they had to hammer nails into the walls is a mystery.

After hostilities, the concert room was returned to its original use, but it seems that the projection room up that short flight of steps was forgotten about. Many years later I was to enter that forgotten room and the sole projector still stood forlornly, pointing out of the single projection porthole.

I have fond memories of being taken to the Works by my parents. It must have been my first association with the pictures. It started me on my lifelong love of cinema and introduced me to all of my heroes. We always sat on the right side of the concert room, with me on a chair by the aisle, with the pub-style round table separating me from my parents. The lights dimmed and the screen became alive with action. My eyes were glued to that screen, with a cream soda firmly clasped in my hand.

I could never understand in those days why the film stopped every little while. I thought it was to allow people to get drinks, but it was because the Works had only one projector. But that did not matter because Bogey Kelsty, better known to us kids as the Chocolate Man, would appear with his large wicker basket of goodies. Mine was always a Mars bar and even in the early part of the war, before the hall was closed, he would still be there with something or other.

One thing that has always remained in my mind about the Works is the picture that hung on a wall at the top of those stairs. It was of a scene from the Battle of Jutland in 1916, with a young boy seaman manning the forward gun of H.M.S. *Chester*. He had been awarded the Victoria Cross posthumously. Why it hung in the club and why it had a profound impression upon me, I have never discovered.

In 1952 I was involved with mobile cinema shows, and I was asked if

I could revive film shows at the Works with some pilot shows. I visited that old projection room with the thoughts of projecting from there, but it was not possible for technical reasons. I did, however, find the old projector still in situ and the early 'talkie' system still intact. Further investigation revealed that I could not bring it back to use.

I did start films again, this time on 16mm, and the revived Sunday lunch shows were popular. I could not continue, however, because I was in full-time projection work in a Kettering cinema.

In 1953 Woodfield Mobile Cinema, operated by Mr. E. Toseland and Mr. E. Sharp, ran a film at the Works on 16mm, but this seems to have been the only other presentation of film in the old Concert Hall.

Nothing remains of the concert room today. It became a fitness centre. When I last visited the town, the 'escape' door of the old projection was still visible, indicating past times. While not a commercial cinema in the true sense, the Works was a sort of sixth cinema in the town and held a special place in the hearts of many who, like me, sat on those hard chairs being enthralled by those lovely old images and a bottle of pop.

Projection and Technical Information

The projector installed, as listed by the late Colin Ball, was a Gaumont Chrono. This is not disputed, however on my visit to the projection room in 1952 the projector was a Gaumont 16 (likely called a Chrono because of the mechanism). It had a front shutter arrangement. I would presume that as a silent projector it was installed as such and had the BA optical soundhead fitted in 1933. The sound system amplifier was British Talking Pictures. There was a rectifier room but this was empty on inspection. The screen was presumably fitted to the back stage wall. There was a set of screen tabs, as I remember.

Miniature Rifle Club & Rifle Band Club

The Miniature Rifle Club situated in Hallwood Road – a modest building adjacent to the Rockingham Road Pleasure Grounds – provided filmed entertainment for its members and associates for a short period. The club had no concert hall and the films were shown in the main bar area, mostly at Sunday lunchtimes in the years from 1948 to 1951.

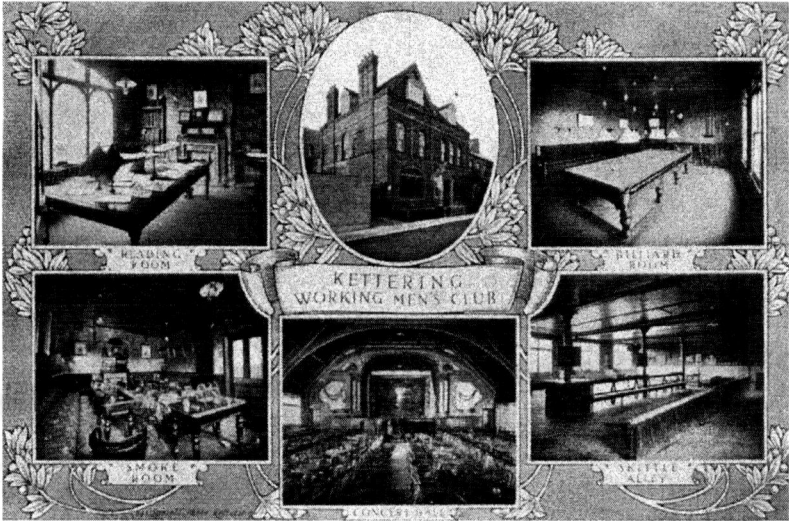

An advertising postcard of the Club
(Photo: D. Wharton)

The building
pictured in 1998
(Photo: D. Wharton)

*The original club building and
the Concert Room (cinema)
(Photo: D. Wharton)*

*Rear of the club
showing the fire escape
door (green) from the
projection room
(Photo: M. Thornton)*

The shows were very popular and even had a serial running in each programme, which ensured the members' attendance weekly. One wonders quite how the films and the general noise in the bar were compatible, but the performances were well received and only ended because of the soaring costs of film hire. Contrary to belief, there was never a projection room purpose-built at the club, and 35mm film was not shown.

Projection

Projection services were provided by Woodleigh Mobile Cinema and operated by Mr. E. Toseland and Mr. H. Sharp. The portable equipment was set up in the Committee Room. The projectors were thought to be CARPENTER 16mm with 1000watt lamp output.

The **Rifle Band Club,** was a two-storey building set back off Havelock Street and a popular Working Men's Club. The concert room occupied much of the upper floor and was used for all manner of functions, providing entertainment for its members and associates.

Films on 16mm were shown there on Sunday evenings between 1948 and 1951. They were the same programme as would have been shown at the Miniature Rifle Cub at lunchtime the same day. The hall could seat around two hundred for the performances. The shows were very popular and ceased for the same reason of escalating film and transit costs.

It is recorded elsewhere that a projection room existed at the club. There was a 'concrete slab' at the rear of the concert room and this was used as a projection base, however there is no evidence that a projection room ever existed or that 35mm films were ever shown.

Projection: Provided by Woodleigh Mobile Cinema.

Town Band Club – Windmill Club

There have been reports that at one time there was a projection room built on the concert room of the town Band Club, set back off the Rockingham Road, and that films were shown there.

Exhaustive research has failed to substantiate that fact and no evidence forthcoming to whether 35mm, or indeed 16mm films, were shown at the club. Therefore, that leaves me with the conclusion that film performances on a regular basis were never provided.

The **Windmill Club** Working Men's Club, on the corner of Edmund Street and Stamford Road, was built around 1935. A spacious premises, and all on ground floor level, it had a very well equipped Concert Hall and, although narrow, widened out at the stage end. It had all the facilities for entertainment, with dressing rooms and modern stage lighting. No film projection facility was built into the hall but it is remembered that films were shown from time to time. The projection equipment was set up at the rear of the hall, and almost certainly used a 16mm mobile projection outfit.

The Wicksteed Park

The Wicksteed Park at Kettering is a very popular playground, and caters for all types of leisure activity and entertainment. First laid down by Charles Wicksteed in 1919, it is reckoned to be Britain's first ever theme park. As all such open-air venues depend upon weather, some indoor provision was provided in the form of a large wooden structure. During WW2, much of the Park's facilities were requisitioned and this was used for storage and never returned to use.

In 1952 a new purpose-built entertainment hall was built on the site. The building had an attractive brick façade, with central entrance doors leading to a small foyer and then to the main hall. There was an adequate stage at the far end, equipped with dressing rooms and stage lighting. A projection room was constructed over the entrance foyer. At the time of opening, it was appropriately named The Coronation Hall.

All sorts of entertainment took place and regular film shows were performed during inclement weather. Mostly for children, the shows consisted of cartoons, comedies and family features. The hall could seat between 300 and 400, the seating being portable. Though not a permanent cinema, it was very popular and served a welcome addition to motion-picture presentation for the town, and therefore deserves a mention.

Projection and Technical Information

Two 35mm projectors were installed in the small projection room. The make of the projectors is not recorded but the installation included a sound system, which also served as the hall's public address facility. Speakers for film sound were situated on stage and the screen was a 'roll-up' type.

Part 5

YARNS, CUSTOMS AND PERSONALITIES

Cinemas have created a lore that endures. In themselves they were a focal point of the neighbourhood they occupied; as important as the public house or the local shop. Workers in the town's manufacturing industries, the shoe factories, the engineering shops, the tanneries and the many other facets of the Kettering economy, could relieve their often drab lives by going to the cinema and being transported into a world created for and portrayed by the cinema. The films, the stars, the spectacle, were all up there on that big screen, and the cinema became temples of egalitarian patronage and social importance. Let us indulge in some tales that make Kettering's cinema heritage.

Silent Cinema

That it never was. What the film may have lacked in audibility was made up for by the ambience within the cinema itself. The thud of the tip-up seats. The click of the piano reading light as it was switched on. The mechanical clatter of the projectors. The rattle of the pianist's rings and bangles as she raised the tempo to the action on the screen. The hiss of the hygienic spray as it was carried around the hall, spelling death to germs and customers' dandruff. The renewed clatter of the tip-up seats as patrons expected THE END to appear, only to recede momentarily as it did not. The rustle of sweet papers and sucked lollipops. The occasional snore.

Kettering screens were certainly no exception. There was always some form of accompaniment to the images on the screen. To be a 'cinema musician', whether solo or in a combination, was not always a pleasant pastime. Not every picture held attention, and at **Vint's Palace** the pianist was encased in a mesh cage as protection from the missiles pelted at them, usually obtained from the market outside.

There would be a more genteel clientele at the **Electric Pavilion** and the **Victoria Picture House,** although there would be moments of audience participation especially if the projector operator got into difficulties. Common to all cinemas was the countdown when the film leader came up on the screen; a practice that can still exist today. The **Empire** had a particular opportunity for audience involvement. The projection portholes were only just above the rear seats of the balcony, and heads would appear on the screen as big black blobs, as well as the odd sign produced by a pair of hands. This was usually greeted by a loud chorus of *sit down,* or something more choice from the audience.

The raked floor of the **Electric Pavilion** was another noise-maker. There was no carpet in the early days. If one sat on the left hand side of the cinema, going to the toilets required walking down to the stage front, across and halfway up the other side. It required one to put the feet down heavily to retain balance on the downward trip, and equally to return. To say that the noise must have sounded like a herd of animals would be understandable.

The **Hippodrome,** and probably other cinemas in town, experimented with the 'sound accompanied picture' by placing 'actors' behind the screen to read from scripts, shouting the words in attempted unison with the action on screen. Suffice to say that the films were mercifully short and simple phrases were used. The actors would speak through large sound horns. Quite popular, too, was the introduction of sound effects.

At the **Hippodrome,** chains were dragged backstage to resemble thunder, and there were other effects with horses hooves and whistles, etc. This was par for this cinema. In its previous role as **Vint's Palace,** the General Manager Arthur Brogden had proved to be an inventive master at this, providing much amusement to the patrons.

The **Victoria Picture House** was not about such antics, but it did have a fine orchestra and, with prestige films, would introduce vocal interludes to parts of the films. When Cecil B. DeMille's film 'The Ten Commandments' (1923) was shown, a full augmented orchestra played the special musical score, enhanced by local artistes singing appropriate arias for the important scenes in the film. Kettering cinemas were never silent.

A reality play

Drama did not only happen on the stage of the old **Avenue Theatre** in Russell Street. During the week of 7th January, 1907, the George Henry Theatre Company were performing the play 'The Sledgehammer' when, on the last night, there was a fracas in the male dressing room. The play concerned two men – brothers – who eventually attack each other with sledgehammers. The actors playing the roles were Arthur Alexander Clark, of Lewisham, and Arthur James Murray, of Walworth. A little before the final performance on the Saturday night, a dispute arose about the use of pegs in the dressing room, and resulted in clothes being thrown around and a blazing row.

Clarke attempted to strike Murray, who was the bigger of the two, and they fell to the floor. Murray produced a knife and stabbed Clark in the abdomen. Clark, not severely injured, continued his performance but collapsed and was taken to hospital. George Henry called the Police, and Murray was arrested. Murray eventually appeared before Kettering Magistrates and was sent to Assizes at Northampton, finally receiving star billing in Bedford Prison.

Bioscope - King of the Cinematograph

Warren East was a well known Kettering photographer and lanternist. He was also in business as a travelling Bioscope showman, touring the area with his lantern and Bioscope shows. Interesting is this advert for his services, dated January 1907, where he declares that his Bioscope show is 'The King of the Cinematograph' and can be engaged for entertainment at bazaars, schools, private parties and similar events.

Songs are illustrated by suitable pictures, but the cinematograph may also be engaged alone. Edison's Grand Concert Phonograph may be engaged separately or together with the cinematograph or if wished the whole Company. For your enjoyment the Company comprises of Mr. Warren East, cinematographist, Mr. William C. Hooper, descriptive lecturer, Mr. Arthur Turner, phonographist and Miss C. Hillier accompanist and vocalist.

How much it would have cost to hire this ensemble is not recorded but, following Warren East's splendid performance at the Victoria Hall six years earlier, this must have been a grand entertainment in those years before cinemas.

Pews In All Parts

In 1935 an odd proposal was publicised in the town, which had interesting repercussions. Church leaders from denominations in Kettering met to witness a demonstration of two types of film projector, prior to an order being placed. The Reverend Cornwell told those gathered that 26 million visited the cinema every week while only three million went to church. He went on to state that the showing of films would not be in competition with cinemas in the town, however there were certain pictures which were no good for children (no-one had bothered to ask them) 'and we will aim to show films which will make children feel, when coming out of OUR shows, that they have learned something'.

Fears were then expressed that if churches were to show films on Sundays, the cinemas might press for Sunday opening. This prompted the Reverend Cornwell to declare that if cinemas were to show films such as those the churches would – and took collections – then they were welcome to open on a Sunday.

It was eventually proposed to show films every Sunday after the evening service. Admission would be free, with a collection. Plans were made to slightly alter the Toller Church Hall in Meeting Lane so that the proposed plan could take place.

There was, of course, much opposition to the plan and it would seem that the venture never took off. The Toller rooms plans were not proceeded with and there was no further reportage in the local press.

(Note: Sunday opening of cinemas did become established a few years later.)

A World Premiere

A typical London premiere took place in Kettering on March 20th, 1951, when a world premiere of the British film 'The Browning Version' (1951) was staged to celebrate the refurbishment of the **Odeon**. The film starred Michael Redgrave as the schoolmaster – the central figure of the Terence Rattigan novel – Jean Kent and Nigel Patrick.

There were crowds in Gold Street and the **Odeon** had been decked with flags, bunting and flowers as befitted the occasion. The highlight of the premiere was the reading from the stage by 17-year-old Brian Smith, a local lad, who had a leading role as one of the schoolboys in the film.

Pow-wow at Kettering Reservation

Publicity stunts were regular features for cinemas, and Kettering cinemas were no exception. March 1926 saw a stunt that was to stir the very hearts of every brave in the reservation when a real Red Indian Chief visited the town. The **Empire** was showing the pot-boiler, 'The Thundering Herd' (1925), which starred Jack Holt, Noah Beery and Indian Chief White Elk. A film to stir the Empire patrons, it had it all – Indian raids, cattle drives, guns spitting, arrows flying, and a little bit of love interest.

To publicise the film, Paramount had despatched White Elk to England to rustle up the local tribes and make sure they attended the big pow-wow in the cinema tepees. He rode into Kettering and tethered his stallion (actually it was a mare from a local horse owner) to the hitching rail at the Empire. From the flat roof of an adjacent shop, he proceeded to perform his tribal dance to the accompaniment of his own hoots and yells, stirring up the patrons as they queued for the film. It is noted that the Swan saloon nearby was serving hostile ranchers and that the local Sheriff, complete with helmet and size tens, managed to keep the peace.

Here Comes Charlie?

If it was Chaplin you wanted to see, then it was nearly always the **Electric Pavilion** where his films were shown. This raises an interesting controversy which has surfaced on more than one occasion in the past. Did Charles Chaplin once come to Kettering to publicise a film? There was an item which appeared in the *Evening Telegraph* in the 1970s and another some years later about this matter.

The first report tells of a house in Wadcroft, No. 30 it seems, which was owned by a Mrs. Susannah Hawthorne, at which Charles Chaplin stayed for two weeks whilst making a personal appearance with the showing of the film, 'Escaped Convict'. It gives no date, but the film is described as 'one of his earlier screen efforts' and talks of the days when he was an almost unknown 'film player'. The report goes on to say that there was not much room in the house in Wadcroft and that he had to sleep with the landlady's two sons in a big iron bed. To advertise the picture, he would walk around the town dressed in a convict's garb, with shoes on the wrong feet. Children waited for hours outside of 30 Wadcroft for him to appear, then followed him around town.

No. 30 Wadcroft (1920s). The house where Chaplin was said to have lodged (Photo: Kettering Leader)

Was it he who stayed at No 30 Wadcroft?

The second report quotes a letter disputing all of this. It infers that it was a look-alike, however yet even another writer stated that he had actually talked to Chaplin and been convinced of the authenticity because of his dress and the fact of his accent being perfect. This letter, however, quotes the film showing as being 'The Prisoner' and the year 1926.

Was it, or was it not Chaplin? It is difficult to say, as there is no further evidence beyond the reports; however, both are doubtful. First the film titles are not recognised and are unlikely to exist. The nearest title which has any similarity is 'The Pilgrim' (1923), which concerns an escaped convict posing as a clergyman. Secondly, Chaplin is not on record as having visited Britain at the time quoted, he being busy filming.

Something probably took place at that time involving a Charles Chaplin film. Was it a very good lookalike doing a publicity stunt for a film we cannot identify? Could anyone really believe that, with his wealth, he would sleep three-in-a-bed in a small terraced house in the centre of town for two weeks? Having said that, should we deprive the writers of these accounts of a probable treasured memory, for as we know anything is possible in the world of cinema?

Boys of the Band

Would you ever have expected to hear a bugle band playing in an operetta? It happened in the **Savoy** way back in 1960. The Kettering and District Theatrical Society staged 'White Horse Inn' at the theatre, and the director decided that she wanted a spectacular welcome as the Emperor Franz-Joseph entered centre stage. Having no military band available, the task was given over to the Kettering Sea Cadet Corps' drum and bugle band, which had quite a substantial reputation for its prowess.

The lads, on cue, with their drum major in the lead, struck up in the foyer of the theatre and marched down each aisle and onto the stage. There they counter-marched before heralding the Emperor with a resounding fanfare. When a drum and bugle band is in full flow, the acoustics are something to reckon with, especially within a theatre. But the audience loved it.

The boys received a standing ovation from the audiences throughout the week and, on the last performance, received a gigantic cake designed as a battleship, which was demolished in minutes in the dressing room after the show. Quite what Benatzky and Stolz would have made of it, is open to question.

Another Film Stunt

I was working at the **Granada** and we were showing 'April Love' (1956), starting on a Monday. Stunts were a major expectation with Granada and good publicity promoting films was foremost, so I got involved in a caper for the film. The story of the film concerned a young man, played by Pat Boone – a heart-throb of the day – who was on probation with the law, and had been sent to his uncle's farm to pay for his crime. It was, in fact, a remake of 'Home In Oklahoma' (1944).

On the Saturday before the opening of the film, a small number of the cinema staff were told to come with jeans and checked shirts as costume. When we assembled, we were confronted by a barrel organ which had been loaned from a local charity. We soon learned that we were to push this organ around the streets during the afternoon, playing songs on its barrel, promoting the film, and collecting money for the local charity whose organ it was. It had been suitably adorned with cut-outs of the stars of the film, with the Granada logo prominently displayed. Quite what this had to do with the actual film was never questioned as we set off on our quest.

Of the group, two people had to push the organ, one turned the handle to play the music, and two more had to walk with collecting buckets. We took it in turns and everything went well throughout the afternoon until the last tour at around four o'clock.

By now we were getting tired, and pushing the quite heavy organ took its strain, not to mention turning the handle almost continuously. Add to that, it had no brakes, thus had to be restrained on undulating roads.

On the last run down Market Street, the inevitable happened. The street was on a hill with a sharp curve halfway down. It was my turn on the handle and I was belting out a cheery tune, when I felt the organ gain speed. Momentarily, the two pushing had faltered and the organ took over. Down the remaining slope of the street it went, my two colleagues doing their best to hold it back. Unable to stop or turn it, and with me now running still turning the handle, it ran off the road and straight through the opened revolving doors of the Royal Hotel at the bottom of the street, much to the astonishment and alarm of the few people sitting in the lounge.

We returned to the cinema, barrel organ in tow, very tired and weary. Unfortunately the Manager did not quite see the funny side of the mishap, but was happy with the money we raised.

Jumping G.I.

Margaret McManus was a cashier at the **Regal** during WW2, and tells of the day a strange incident took place in the cinema. During a short interval in the programme, an American soldier sitting in the circle suddenly left his seat and stood at the front, looking down into the stalls. Without any indication, he climbed up on to the circle front and leapt, landing on a lady sitting directly below in the stalls. He was not seriously hurt, but the woman he landed on suffered two broken legs. She was taken to hospital and he was arrested. The reason for his jump was never explained but rumour had it that he was either drunk, drugged, or deeply disturbed, though none of that was ever disclosed.

3-D or not 3-D

As mentioned, the **Granada** had most of the Natural Vision 3-D productions, and I remember one afternoon quite vividly. We were showing 'Charge at Feather River' (1953), with full Warnerphonic stereo sound. I had gone down to the foyer to get our jug of tea and went back to the projection room via the circle. Passing through, I noticed an elderly lady who at first sight looked to be asleep, however as I passed her she looked at me and I noticed she was not wearing the 3-D spectacles. I approached her with caution, not wanting to startle her, and politely asked her why she was not wearing the glasses, as she could not see the picture without them.

Her reply both startled and amused me, for she looked up and whispered, '*Oh those. I don't wear glasses, you know. I can see quite*

132

well without them so I gave them to the nice lady as I came in. Thank you for your concern, young man.' I left her without further comment.

Alah Bukh, a Kettering lad, admits that on one or two occasions he was 'asked' to leave the **Regal.** He recalls that if they were showing a sloppy musical picture, we would be on our worst behaviour. Should there be a Western or Humphrey Bogart film running, then we were good boys. Of course, if we had no money, we got in through the back exit doors only to be thrown out through the front doors when caught. Our favourite trick was to pool our funds and then one or two would pay to go in. Once in, it was a visit to the toilet and opening the push-bar to let in the rest. Everyone then came out of the toilet in dribs and drabs.

The **Empire** had double seats at the back of the balcony. And we would scramble for these and then lay across them. Of course when we got older, they found other uses. That cinema was easy, but at the **Odeon** there was a 'four square rigged' bloke on the front and there was no fooling with him.

One Sunday night we were sitting in the front rows, waiting for the film to start. One of our gang had a brother who was an airman and he'd just got back from North Africa. He had brought some bananas home and this lad had brought one with him to show us. We had not seen such a sight for many years, if at all, and it caused quite a commotion with us climbing over seats to see this wonder. Suddenly the 'four square commissionaire' was confronting us, along with Mr. Dawson, the manager, and we found ourselves in Gold Street with a three week ban.

On another occasion we again were in the **Odeon,** occupying the front seats. The film was quite good but failing to hold our attention. Suddenly a number of bats, at least that is what we thought they were, were flying back and forth in front of the screen. This caused hilarious reaction from us and we began waving our arms and shouting. As always, we were quickly shown the door.

Hail, Hail, Rock and Roll

Many still can remember the glorious one-night stands staged at the **Granada** during the late 1950s and early 1960s. Granada Theatres had organised some of the first touring Pop-star shows, and Kettering was well served by them. Each star-packed show came around every few weeks. Stars like Cliff Richard, Tommy Steele, Billy Fury, Gene Vincent, Eddie Cochran, The Searchers, Marty Wilde, Lonnie Donegan, Adam Faith, The Rolling Stones; they all appeared on the Granada stage. The stars were supported by up-and-coming bands and artistes. Just about every British pop star played the cinema.

The first show was at 6pm, with a second one timed for 8.30pm. The shows lived up to their branding as a 'pop package' and were fast adrenalin, exciting productions, performing non-stop, with a headline act featured to close each half of the show. Many stars would be billed on the same programme. Such was the demands of the crowd that the second show would rarely get underway until 9pm, and the last show often ended around midnight.

Front stalls were 10 shillings (50p), and then 7 shillings and sixpence (35p), and 5 shillings (25p). The circle was similarly priced. The noise was tremendous. There were quieter shows with Mark Wynter, Matt Munroe, Max Bygraves, and Acker Bilk. Such was the level of audience participation that additional speakers had to be flown from the ceiling to serve those in the circle. Nothing quite like this had been seen in Kettering before and it was greatly appreciated, especially by the young people of the town who probably would never have witnessed their pop idols in the flesh without these shows.

Personalities

Archie Mason was the Chief Projectionist at the **Gaumont**. He started in the cinema in 1915 as a 'chocolate boy' for seven shillings a week. After service in the Great War, he returned to the cinema, working as an usher, and graduated to the job of a projectionist, becoming the chief many years later.

When the **Gaumont** closed in 1959, he moved to the **Odeon** in Kettering and also Corby. His wife, Florence, worked as cashier and she was also first violinist in the pit orchestra at the **Victoria Picture House,** where they first met. Archie was one of the most respected cinema figures in the town. He was again in the news when, in 1998, his wife discovered a short piece of film of the RMS *Titanic* he had purchased many years earlier, which was brought to light with publicity for the acclaimed film 'Titanic' (1997), when it was shown in Kettering.

Lance Roberts, Chief Projectionist at the **Odeon** and it is believed a projectionist at the **Victoria Picture House** for many years, was well respected locally. There are many stories about how Lance ran the projection room at the Odeon. The one chosen here may or not have been true, but it is a nice story.

Near to the projection room were situated fire buckets – one filled with water, the other sand. Lance would have the water changed weekly, the sand 'combed', and the outsides of the buckets polished to a high sheen. His projection room was spotless and run to a high standard as befitted the theatre.

Another spotless projection room was at the **Regal** and **Granada**, under the command of Chief **Eric Walters**. Eric came to the Regal from London; though the date is not known, it is thought to be at its opening in 1936. He had begun his career as a projectionist at the old Stoll Theatre in the days of silent film. Eric was quite a character and I got to know him well as my chief when I worked there. He did his job in a quiet and efficient way. As a projectionist in the Royal Navy, I was taught about showing pictures, but Eric taught me how to show them. He was a showman and even with the Granada corporate image, he still managed those little extra touches reminiscent of the old Regal.

A projectionist's job was an 'art' for, as Eric would say, it put the icing on the cake when showing the picture, even if the cake was a little sad at times. Varied and innovative, it could be exciting and tedious, but always unpredictable, and it is sad that today the profession – because that is what it was – is lost forever, due to technology and fiscal demands.

For the other cinemas, there is little record of the projection or front of house staff, as it seems there was a turnover of people through the years. Noted though, is that Bernard Ridley and Peter Cowan were both at the **Empire** as chief projectionists at some time, and Alan Gray was similarly employed at **The Studios.**

Up front and out front, the owners and managers of the cinemas were the epitome of autocracy, most ruling their charges with efficiency and flair. Kettering cinemas had their quota of the best, and one or two of the lesser variety. The owners expected good business, whether they be a national chain or local independent, and those expectations had to be realised. For the circuits, this was the responsibility of the manager. The independents would either employ a manager or manage themselves.

Leo Vint put **Arthur Brogden** in charge when he opened the **Electric Palace.** Brogden was a shrewd man and wooed the audiences to the new cinema. His job was not too difficult at first, because there was little opposition. He was an ambitious man and not too well liked. He was, however, innovative and brought real flair, standing out front in full view of the noisy market and the occasional consequences. When Leo Vint sold the cinema, Brogden moved to work elsewhere.

When the **Coliseum** opened, **William Jackman** was the manager. He was heralded by the press as a man of wonderful enterprise. He had his work cut out as he now had competition from three other enterprises. Regardless, he brought success to the theatre, though he seems to have left after a while.

Mr. J. Needham was manager when the **Victoria Picture House** opened and he remained so for many years. A small man, well groomed and dressed, he could always be found front of house presenting the image of a well-run cinema. He was, however, not very communicative with his staff, had little rapport with them and an inability to take people along with him. He was a worrier and allowed his problems to add to his reticence. For all that, he took the cinema though its primary years and was well liked by the patrons.

Jack Sherwood, from Tipton in Staffordshire, married the daughter of the original owner of the **Coliseum** and took over the cinema in 1932. He established himself as a showman next to none, and became a real cinema personality. He was a tall 'man about town', slightly bent in stature, with sleek, shiny dark hair and was the essence of the times. He was always immaculately dressed and it was said that he looked as if he had stepped out of a Burtons' window.*

* *Burtons was a bespoke tailor with a nationwide chain of shops*

Mr. JACK SHERWOOD,
Managing Director of the new Savoy
Cinema Luxury Theatre.

Mrs. JACK SHERWOOD,
whose father the late Mr. Frank
Payne built the original Coliseum in
Russell Street

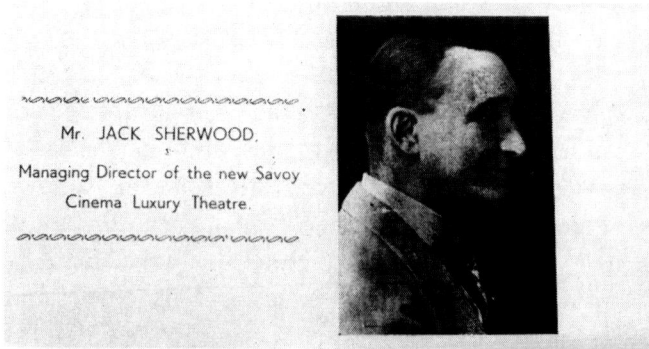

Top: Jack Sherwood/Bottom: Mrs. Sherwood
(Photo: from Savoy opening programme)

He always struck an imposing figure as he stood in the Coliseum foyer. He had an eminence about him and he was extremely likeable, though modest and rather diffident, but his shyness did not affect his drive to make the theatre the leading entertainment house in town. After the old 'Col' was destroyed, he was responsible for much of the building of the **Savoy.**

Mrs. Sherwood was equally flamboyant. She could have been mistaken for a movie queen. Dressed in the latest London fashions, and with her white make-up and heavily rouged cheeks, she would arrive at the cinema with her husband, trailing an air of elegance and royalty. Her distinctive appearance was enhanced further by her scarlet lipstick which, when applied, looked as though she was blowing a kiss.

Along with the Sherwoods, there was **Harold Jackson.** He was well dressed, had dark wavy hair and bore the appearance of a matinee idol. He could often be found walking about Kettering in his suede shoes, his top coat draped around his shoulders in a showbiz manner. He was a good manager, ever in at the thick of things, a likeable person, always on the lookout for the extraordinary to present on the theatre's stage.

A manager well respected in the town was **Bert Dawson,** who started his cinema career at the **Coliseum** and was musical director there for a while. When the 'Col' went over to pictures, he moved to the **Empire** as manager. A move to further his career saw him become manager at the **Odeon Corby** in 1940. He moved as manager to the **Odeon Kettering** in 1942, and remained there until retirement. He was a very efficient leader of the staff and was alert to his patrons' likes and dislikes. He did seem to have a different approach to boys, as I recall.

One Sunday evening, we were in the front rows as usual and a little restless, as one hour of Victor Sylvester was hard to bear. Staff were having none of it and we got marched to Bert's office. He read the riot act to us and then stood us outside of his office for all to see until the film was nearly ready to start. We stood quietly until told to return. If we had not been, then out we would have gone. You did not mess with Bert.

The first manager at the **Regal** was **L. Morely-Clarke.** Like Jackson, he was a flamboyant character and dressed like a movie mogul, with a smart double-breasted suit and a wide-brimmed hat. He might even be seen with the odd cigar. He was another popular manager, treating his patrons in a 'regal' fashion. During WW2 the manager was **Jack Goldy,** who came from London but had settled in Kettering. Flamboyant he certainly was not. Staff regarded him with respect, but were not over-fond of him. He ran the cinema well enough, but had little truck with boys.

When buying our ten penny tickets, we always tried to evade his glare, looking innocent as we descended the steps, past his office, to the stalls. His son, **Emmanuel (Manny) Goldy,** was the assistant manager; a job he did not particularly relish, but had little option but to do as he was told. What happened to Jack Goldy is unknown, but Manny was working as the chief projectionist at the **Empire** in 1947. In Granada days the managers included Mr. **Palmer** and Mr. **Bush,** both remembered for the stunts Granada used to pull in the town.

Other managers remembered having charge of Kettering's cinemas were Messrs. **Brett, Barry, Cooke** and **Shepheard** at the **Odeon. Maurice Lee** was managing the **Savoy,** though the dates are obscure. The story goes that he loved Mars bars and could be found at slack moments perched on a radiator, munching way at a bar, only to slip away to his office quietly if potential trouble loomed. **Joseph Lee** (any connection, I know not) managed the **Empire** at one time, before eventually owning the cinema.

What of the COMMISSIONAIRES? Those astute fellows that would walk the queues, keeping them in order and shouting out the seats available. A few have been discovered. **Pop Turner** saw war service before he worked at the **Electric Pavilion** in 1919. He permeated his air of authority from those marble steps, later moving across the road to the plush **Victoria Picture House.** At the **Coliseum** was **Harry Ball,** of whom it was said he was more popular than the stars who trod the boards. To be invited to see his pet parrot was a treat for good children, and the feathered creature became equally as famous.

The **Regal** had '**Pop**'. We never knew his real name, but he was a real character. He was quite strict with youngsters but he was well liked. If you were a 'good un', he would let you in of an afternoon if there was a Humphrey Bogart or James Cagney film showing, but woe betide if you were foolish enough to mess about. In **Granada** days, I seem to remember a chap by the name of **Floyd** who did the job while I was there, but the man who had the saddest task of all was **Harold Carpenter,** who was the last to wear the braid. He saw the closure of the cinema.

Those loveable characters are no longer found today, except perhaps in heritage cinemas.

PART 6

THE YEARS
OF WAR

The importance of cinema during the two world wars of the 20th Century are well documented. Never before had an entertainment industry marshalled so much energy and proliferation to provide entertainment and information for the masses.

What of the role of Kettering cinemas in these conflicts? A glimpse first into the years from 1914 to 1918. Little is written, but the two D.W. Griffith films, 'Birth of A Nation' (1915) and 'Intolerance' (1916), were shown at the **Electric Pavilion** to packed houses in those years. Similarly, at the **Victoria Hall** crowds were paying up to see Mary Pickford in 'Tess of Storm Country' (1915) and 'Pride of the Clan' (1917).

The Christmas of 1914 saw little change in the programming at the **Electric Pavilion.** It had been open for a little over eighteen months and had a clientele used to its rousing programmes. Showing was 'The Call' (1914), starring the then raving beauty of Vitagraph, Clara Kimbell-Young, supported by 'A Christmas Carol' (1914), one of the Vitagraph series of Charles Dickens' tales.

Starting on Boxing Day, the cinema was showing 'Under Two Flags' (1914), starring Alan Hale. It was one of the last to be produced by Biograph. As for the only other cinema, **The Palace** (formerly Vint's Palace), they had variety and were advertising 'pictures from the Front Line'.

The cinematograph was bringing information to the public in a way never before possible, and every showing included an 'actuality' usually by the 'newsreels' of the day, such as Topical Budget and Gaumont Graphic.

Sunday, September 3rd, 1939, war was declared and it was announced that all places of entertainment were to close with immediate effect. Many of the things we took for granted and held dear, ceased. Going to the pictures was one of these. This decree was, in effect, a move to protect the populace because, if what had been the trend with other countries happened here, our towns and cities could expect bombing and the government did not want heavy civilian casualties.

As the days passed, such threats were not imminent and the government, realising the importance entertainment had on keeping up public morale, permitted reopening at the discretion of proprietors. Cinemas across the country were open within hours. For theatres it was more difficult, because many actors were reservists and were called up, causing shows to fold.

Kettering's cinemas were duly closed on Monday, September 4th, and remained dark. With the lifting of the order during that week, reopening took place the following Monday, September 11th by agreement. There were, however, imposed operational times which meant they were open every afternoon and remained so until 10pm, at which time they must close. This pattern remained throughout the years until 1945.

The area was considered relatively safe from air attacks and very quickly received thousands of evacuees. Then came the armed forces and the wartime airfields. Later the area received personnel from all the Allied nations, and then the Americans. The town was bursting at the seams. Cinemas were the main entertainment. Never had they experienced such a wide potential audience, and they rose to the occasion magnificently.

At first there was the Central Hall and The George Hotel Ballroom for dancing, but these were eventually taken over by the government, as was the Working Men's Club concert hall.

No longer did the neons shine out from the Regal and the other cinemas to coax us into their interiors. In the beginning, one could hardly tell they were open. Entrances were darkened and windows entirely blacked, with only little slits to see through. Once inside, however, it was business as usual. The threat of air raids did not seem to deter picture-goers. Wartime reminders were all around, with taped-up windows and air raid warning signs such as at the Regal, which had a large illuminated sign by the side of the stage which informed when there was an air raid warning.

It was still possible to have an ice cream. Eldorado was available, as was Lyons and Walls, but you could not tell the difference. Sweets could be obtained with your coupons.

At night, queuing outside was in complete darkness and the Commissionaire would loom from the blackness with a small torch to report seat availability. Shows finished by ten o'clock and the last buses, usually only one, carried home the remaining patrons; their dim slits of headlamp lights hardly piercing the blackness.

Very soon there was a move to get the cinemas open on Sundays. The need was great now, especially as the only relaxation on the Sabbath were the public houses. National emergency held sway and, despite opposition from the usual sources, cinemas would open on a Sunday but the programme could not start until 7pm. Doors would open at 6pm and that was the time you had to be there if you wanted to get in. The films shown were always repeats.

The Sunday celebrity concerts continued as they had always had done at the **Regal** and **Savoy**. Many top stars of the era, especially the popular wartime dance bands, trod the stages of those cinemas with the regular concerts. Sandy Powell appeared at the Regal in January 1940, and in April Harry Roy and his band presented a full musical production 'Youth In Rhythm', in which over twenty musical acts were staged.

Live shows were the main entertainment provision of the **Savoy**. Kettering benefited from the closure of many London theatres. Top stage acts came to town and, from all accounts, the stars loved to perform on the Savoy stage, which was as big as many of the London counterparts. One of the first big shows was 'Carry On Kettering', which had a host of stars, including George Elrick and Len Young.

Meanwhile, the cinemas in Kettering were enjoying a period of first release films, the same time as they were being exhibited in London. In addition to entertaining the masses, cinemas were in the forefront of helping the war effort.

In January 1940 the management of the **Savoy** were announcing help for the Kettering Poor Children and Evacuees Wartime Clothing Fund, by arranging collections between performances all of that month. The **Regal** ran the Kettering Halfpenny Shoe Fund every Friday night for a season. Collections of money and materials were common-place at all cinemas, and when the special war effort weeks came around, the cinemas became miniature exhibition halls. The **Regal** displayed a Lancaster gun turret for Wings For Victory Week, and for Warship Week a full replica of a warship bridge.

I remember, as a Sea Cadet, collecting every evening on a week that the **Regal** was showing – for a second time – the acclaimed film about H.M.S. *Kelly,* 'In Which We Serve' (1942), and as a double feature, 'Lady Hamilton' (1941), aka 'That Hamilton Woman'. The collection was for the Training Ship *Arethusa,* which was an establishment which looked after orphaned and wayward boys.

Each year a gentleman, I cannot recall his name, would visit the cinema to raise money for the cause and he would always sing the same ballad, 'A Batchelor Gay Am I' (I doubt you could get away with that now) to a lukewarm applause, but the cadets would be busy sending the collecting tins up and down the rows of patrons – and the best of all got to see the picture free.

Many people went to the pictures every week, maybe twice. Memories, too, as we stood in those queues. The world was around us with lots and lots of service people, many from other lands, and we learned more there than we ever did at school. We were introduced to the Americans, who were either based on the nearby airfield or billeted in town. The bubble gum and chocolate was dispensed around to the kids, and the tales were told.

Once Sunday, whilst standing in the **Pavilion** queue, we were next to a group of black American soldiers. We got along well with them, as we had seen virtually no black people before this time, let alone spoken to a black man. Everything was fine until the arrival of two S.P.s (American

Service Police), who immediately ordered the black soldiers out of the queue and sent them to the rear, which meant they would probably not have got into the cinema. We could not understand why this was and it had a profound effect upon me.

Towards the end of the war, there were Italian and German P.O.W.s out on 'parole' and many people were moved in locally to do war work in the factories and ironstone pits. Kettering was certainly a cosmopolitan community and the cinemas took up the challenges, keeping the populace entertained. By the end of 1945, we were about to enter a new era.

Part 7

ON STAGE
AND
SCREEN

What did the patrons pay to see on the screen or stage of Kettering's entertainment houses? To record that would take volumes, interesting though it would be. Competition was always keen and this ensured good business. A broad aspect, then, will perhaps suffice.

In the early days **Vint's Palace** had little competition with presenting the Cinematograph. At Christmas 1912 it was variety, starring The Bouncing Dillons as the top act. On the screen 'A Peep Behind the Scenes' (1912), a saga of the stage in five parts, and some two reel shorts. At the **Hippodrome,** the show for Christmas 1920 the main feature was 'Broken Melody', starring Martin Harvey, described in the Press review as 'of wringing the very last tear from the audience'. In support was a Chaplin short, 'Charlic's Night Out', aka 'Rounders' (1914), which also starred Roscoe 'Fatty' Arbuckle, and the last episode of the serial 'Lightning Raider'.

Countering the opening of the Coliseum in 1910, **the Victoria Hall** staged 'High Varieties', featuring Bosanquet-the Human Violin, and some supporting two reelers. With the conversion to the **Victoria Picture House,** it became the premier cinema in town, as was realised by showing the top box office films, such as 'Peg O' My Heart' (1922), starring the great American actress Laurette Taylor.

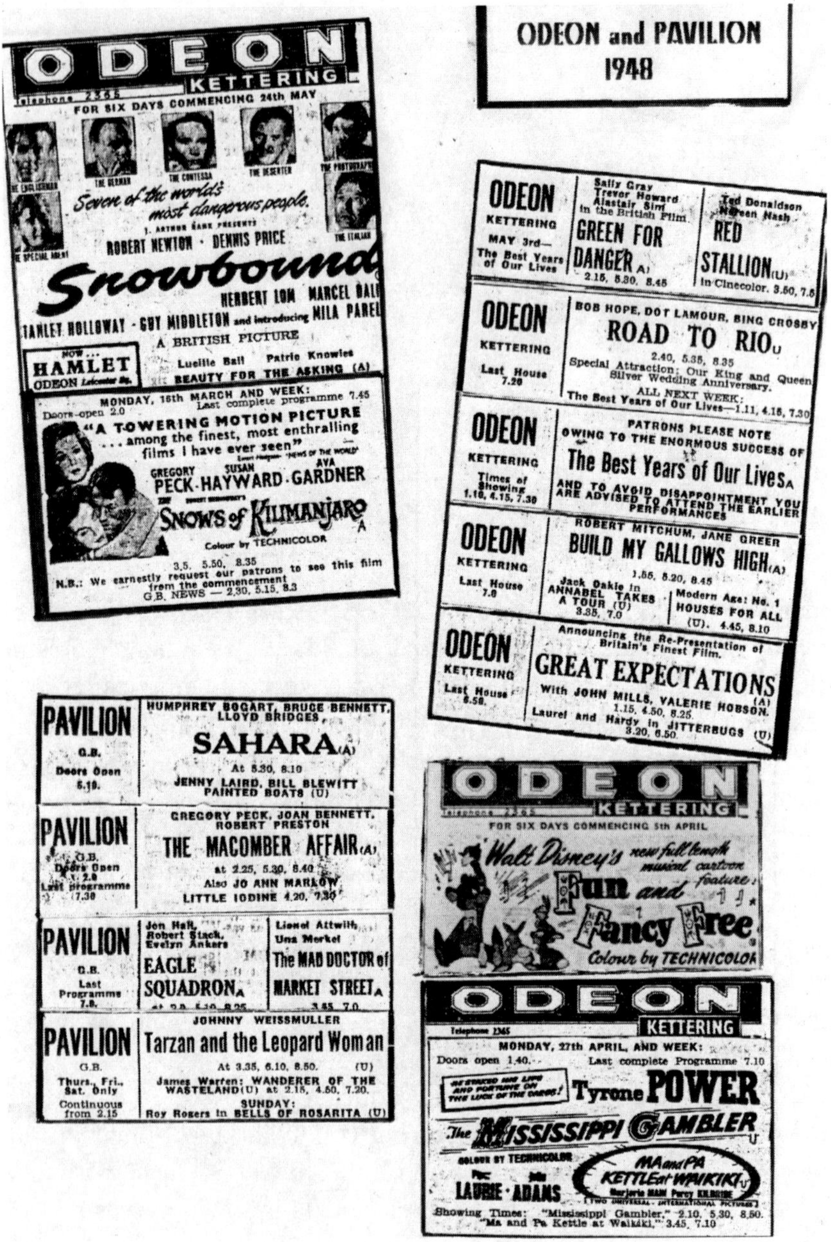

Typical Odeon and Pavilion programming, 1940s

First weeks at the
GRANADA

AND ... ONLY AT **GRANADA**

GRANADA
"HILARIOUS"
Daily Graphic
"Can't imagine finer screen entertainment"
News of the World
BURT LANCASTER
The Crimson Pirate
TECHNICOLOR

GRANADA Last Program 7.35 — Two Complete Programs: 6.30 and 7.35. ROBERT MONTGOMERY, ROSALIND RUSSELL — NIGHT MUST FALL. THE THREE STOOGES EVEN AS I.O.U. (U)

GRANADA Last Program 7.20 — It's Revised—Just how you will like it. INGRID BERGMAN, GARY COOPER FOR WHOM THE BELL TOLLS. In Technicolor. 2.10, 5.10, 8.10. The Merry Musical MINSTREL DAYS | This is Exciting Spills For Thrills (U)

GRANADA Last Program 7.20 — Killer v. Killer James Cagney George Raft EACH DAWN I DIE (A) 2.45, 5.45, 8.45 | A Roaring Western Dennis Morgan, Wayne Morris BAD MEN OF MISSOURI (A) 1.30, 4.30, 7.30

GRANADA Thurs. Fri. Sat. Open 1.25 Last programme 7.20 — IT'S THE TOPS FOR LAUGHS .... GEORGE COLE, NADIA GRAY TOP SECRET (U) 2.45, 5.50, 8.50 Richard Todd introduces ELSTREE STORY (U) 1.30, 4.30, 7.30

GRANADA LAST PROGRAM 7.5 — TWO BIG FEATURES Ray Milland MINISTRY OF FEAR (A) 5.30, 8.15 | Jim Bannon MISSING JUROR (A) 7.5

GRANADA Last Program 7.55 — Tears Glamour from the Gangster—Ruthless, Devastating RICHARD ATTENBOROUGH BRIGHTON ROCK (A) 1.25, 3.50 6.20, 8.45 SCRAPBOOK FOR 1922 (U)—Commentary by John Snagge

GRANADA Last Program 7.20 — TYRONE POWER, MAUREEN O'HARA THE BLACK SWAN (A) 2.55, 5.55, 8.55. In Technicolor It Couldn't Happen Happier JACK CARSON, JANIS PAIGE LOVE AND LEARN (U) 1.15, 4.30, 7.30

GRANADA Last Program 7.20 — MARGARET JOHNSTON, DULCIE GRAY, and introducing Kieron Moore A MAN ABOUT THE HOUSE (A) 2.40, 5.40, 8.40 SMOKY, MICHAEL WHALEN, SHADOW JACK LONDON'S SIGN OF THE WOLF (U) 1.30, 4.30, 7.30

GRANADA Last Program 7.10 — The Full Screen Version of the Sensational B.B.C. Serial (in Technicolor) THE FOUR FEATHERS (A) JOHN CLEMENTS, RALPH RICHARDSON 1.50, 5.5, 8.25 A Technicolor Tour Mack Sennett's MUSICAL MOVIE. KEYSTONE HOTEL LAND (U) EXTRA! TRAFFIC WITH THE DEVIL (A)

GRANADA Last Program 6.45 — Could You Forgive? ANN SHERIDAN LEW AYRES ZACHARY SCOTT THE UNFAITHFUL (A) 1.35, 5.0, 8.30 | Headmaster of Fun WILL HAY THE GHOST OF ST. MICHAEL'S 3.35, 7.5

GRANADA Last Program 7.25 — Swashbuckling Adventure in Technicolor LARRY PARKS, ELLEN DREW THE SWORDSMAN (A) 3.5, 6.0, 8.50 Ted Donaldson, "Rusty," the Wonder Dog THE SON OF RUSTY (U) 1.50, 4.45, 7.35

GRANADA Last Program 7.20 — Thrilling Drama! Errol Flynn Barbara Stanwyck CRY WOLF (A) 2.45, 5.50, 8.55 | Slap-Stick Comedy. Red Skelton MERTON OF THE MOVIES (U) 1.20, 4.35, 7.30

First few weeks film fare at the Granada

Years later at the **Odeon,** 'Wages of Fear' (1953) was showing the week of the closing of the Empire. Showing that week at the **Gaumont** was Bob Hope in 'Casanova's Night Out' (1954); at the **Savoy** 'Jack Slade', starring Mark Stevens, billed as exceptionally violent at the time; and the **Granada** was filling the auditorium with John Wayne dodging the arrows and bullets in Warner Bros. fourth film in Natural Vision 3-Dimension, 'Hondo' (1953). Those not in the cinemas or lamenting the closure of the Empire, were probably watching TV

At the **Coliseum** during Christmas 1912, there were pictures on the silver screen billed as 'The Eight Commandment in five parts' (1912), supported by 'A Just Verdict' (1911) and a Gaumont Graphic newsreel.

In September 1920 the **Electric Pavilion** was showing a momentous saga in five parts, 'Riders of the Purple Sage' (1919), from the book by Zane Grey and starring William Farnum. A remake of this film was shown at the Pavilion in 1925; this time starring Tom Mix. That version was filmed in a wide-screen process and shown in that format at the cinema. Christmas 1923 saw Richard Denny (a heart-throb of the day) in the boxing epic 'The Abysmal Brute' (1923), supported by the romantic drama 'Till We Meet Again' (1923).

When the **Regal** opened on Boxing Day 1936, the **Gaumont Pavilion** was screening Will Hay in 'Windbag the Sailor' (1936), and The **Odeon** had 'The Man Who Could Work Miracles' (1936), starring Roland Young. At the **Coliseum** Dick Powell, Joan Blondell and Ruby Keeler were starring in the musical 'Colleen' (1936). The **Empire** was doing a re-run of a popular British film, 'Annie Laurie' (1936), starring Will Fyffe.

In contrast, January 1973 saw a very different style of cinema fare. The **Granada** was wooing potential patronage with a double helping of James Bond, running 'Goldfinger' (1964) and 'You Only Live Twice' (1967) as a double-feature programme, and at **The Studio** there was another double helping, this time of titillation with 'Language of Love' (1972) and 'Do You Believe In Swedish Sin?' (1972).

What of that little 'cinema' at the Working Men's Club? For the weekend in January 1938, 'Barbary Coast' (1935), starring Edward G. Robinson, was screened on Saturday night, and a Concert on the Sunday evening. Sunday lunchtime 'Devil and the Deep' (1932), starring Charles Laughton and Tallulah Bankhead, was screened.

To illustrate the range of entertainment that was available, the following panel has been constructed from research for the week the Savoy opened in 1938 and the following week.

* * *

Week of 23rd May
EMPIRE All the week 'Roaring Timber' Richard Dix

===

REGAL All the week 'It Can't Last Forever' Ralph Bellamy
'It's All Yours' Madeline Carroll Mischa Auer
On Stage: The Silver Sax Six
Sunday Sidney Kite and his Orchestra

===

PAVILION All the week 'Angel' Marlene Dietrich Herbert Marshall

===

ODEON All the week 'Riding On Air' Joe E. Brown

===

SAVOY Opening week On Stage: Troise & his Mandoliers & full company

===

WORKING MEN'S CLUB
Saturday 'Laurel & Hardy Murder Case' and shorts
Sunday (lunch) 'The Informer' Victor McLaglen
Sunday eve Concert
    *

Week of 30th May
EMPIRE Mon-Wed 'Vengeance' Wendy Barry
Thurs-Sat 'Unknown Ranger' Frank McHugh

===

REGAL All the week 'Heidi' Shirley Temple

===

PAVILION All the week 'Second Honeymoon' Tyrone Power Loretta Young

==

ODEON Mon-Wed 'Last Adventurers' Kay Walsh
Thurs-Sat 'She Asked For It' William Carson

==

SAVOY Mon-Wed 'Double Wedding' William Powell Myrna Loy
Thurs-Sat 'Maytime' Jeanette McDonald Nelson Eddy

==

WORKING MEN'S CLUB
Saturday Shorts
Sunday lunch 'Devil Horse' Noah Beery Harry Carey
Sunday eve 'Footlight Parade' James Cagney Joan Blondell

***

Part 8

THE LITTLE GEMS
THE CINEMAS OF BURTON LATIMER DESBOROUGH ROTHWELL FINEDON IRTHLINGBOROUGH & THRAPSTON

Now part of the greater environment of Kettering, it is fitting that the cinemas of the surrounding towns are worthy of inclusion in this book. Their cinemas were never a threat to the big houses of their neighbour, but they were patronised and loved by those who attended them and those who ran them. All have passed into other things, but the stories of these little gems are fascinating, and thanks go to those who have contributed to the account of their existence.

1. ELECTRIC PALACE/BENTLEY'S/OHIO Burton Latimer.

'What's on at Watt's?'

That catchy little slogan was the keyword to picture-goers in the small town of Burton Latimer on the outskirts of Kettering, along the

A6 trunk road. Alfred Watts coined the phrase when he took over the Electric Palace in 1924, but the story starts ten years earlier. Local shoe manufacturers, Joseph Westley and Henry Whitney, joined forces with plumbing engineer A.G. Miller and formed a company – the Burton Latimer Electric Palace Company – with seven other local people, each contributing one hundred and fifty pounds. They built the cinema in 1914, set back off the High Street behind what was then a coffee house and a public hall. The cinema was named **The Electric Palace** and incidentally was the only cinema to retain its original name for most of its life. It opened on an unrecorded date in August 1914.

Entrance to the cinema was from the High Street through an arch

Entrance to the Palace, 1985
(Photo: Ashley Whyatt)

of Romanesque design, constructed of masonry. THE PALACE was etched in the arch and the stone buttresses each bore a large electric globe for illumination. Publicity panels were fixed to each buttress and the entrance had two heavy wooden gates. The cinema entrance was reached by a climb which became useful to accommodate queues, though unfortunately not under cover.

The cinema was designed by architect R.J. Williams, of Kettering, to a high standard of spaciousness and comfort. Entering the foyer, the pay desk was immediately to hand and the doors to the auditorium were to the left and right. The cinema seated 500 and was approximately 52ft long and 37ft Wide. The rake from the

152

rear to the screen was around three feet. The front three rows were wooden forms. From those to the last ten rows were green leather tip-up seats, and the remainder were red plush. Twelve 'porthole' type windows, six each side, admitted light into the auditorium, and the walls were tinted with a dark coloured dado and the remainder of the plasterwork was white.

An earlier view of the cinema in busy years, 1960
(Photo: Ashley Whyatt)

The cinema was built with its own electricity generating plant and was heated by a new 'high flow' system, for which A.G. Miller had some responsibility, no doubt. It was a much improved heating system of the day.

While opening in August, publicity for the cinema programmes was not forthcoming until the week of November 2nd and that might be accrued as the official opening. The programme was for a split week, Monday to Wednesday with 'Zigomar' (1914), a crime melodrama starring Paul Brochet; the comedy 'Mrs. Finch and Nephew Billy' (1913); the drama 'Pure Puritive Model' (1912), and 'Senators Bill' (1914). Two other pictures completed the bill, 'Barnyard Firtation' (1913) and 'Politeness Pays' (1913), both Keystone comedies, and 'newsreel' pictures from the Front were shown.

Thursday to Saturday the programme offered 'The Honour of the Law' (1914), 'Seagull' (1913), 'Murray's Wedding Present' (nkn), 'Sandy and Shorty' (1913), 'Start Something' (1913) and 'Pimple Pinched'(1912), and the latest news from the Front. It should be remembered that cinema performances in those day comprised of relatively short films, often only one or two reels in length.

Of this official opening night, the report was laudatory, saying, '*the opening of the new Picture House in Burton Latimer, the Electric Palace, has seen its popularity increase by leaps and bounds. It is attractive with its curved arch and electric lamps cast a flood of light over the High Street. Once inside one is aware of its comfort.*'

There is a report also that a British-made 'Indomitable' projector was installed and that it played the pictures clearly and steadily on the screen. The report continued, '*this was no doubt also to the operator who knew his work well with no lengthy delays between the pictures and credit is due to Mr. W. Miller who played the pianoforte selections enhancing the scenes portrayed on the screen.*'

That projectionist was Mr. Mack Goodman, who by day worked as a painter and decorator for A.G. Miller. The pianist, Wilfred Miller, was brother of A.G. Miller, and his wife was cashier. 'Tut' Clipstone replaced Mack Goodman as projectionist eventually, and later pianists were Wilf Sturman, Cecil Hickman and Ada Wood. The whole operation was very much a family affair; even the directors' wives were employed in the pay desk, selling tickets.

Group photograph of elderly patrons at one of the special treats arranged during the early years. The publicity behind cannot be for the Palace
(Photo: Not confirmed. Thought to be A.G. Miller)

Seat prices were 3d., 6d., 9d., 1shilling, and 1shilling and 3d. The two latter prices were for the leather seats and the plush seats. The programmes changed twice weekly and remained so until 1924. In the early days the local policeman would visit the cinema nightly to see that order was being kept. Other people involved were Ernie and George Potter, Arthur Bray, Tom and Blanche Bailey, who also doubled as a sales lady during the intervals.

Monthly film programme for July, 1959
(Photo: Ashley Whyatt)

Shows were at 8pm Monday to Friday, and 2.30pm, 7pm and 9pm on Saturday. The cinema also staged concerts and was used for other events in the town. When children's treats were held, Mr. J. Coles, a local shoe manufacturer, and hairdresser Jack Benford would recite stories and hand out an orange and a bag of sweets. Jack also wrote for the *Evening Telegraph* as 'Simon Strait'.

A serial was almost always shown, the popular ones being, 'Trail of the Octopus', 'The Green Arrow' and, of course, the Pearl White series. So the cinema remained until 1922 when it was taken over by David Strutley, and then in 1924 it was sold to Alfred Watts.

The Watts family also owned the Regent cinema at Finedon and the Picturedrome at Irthlingborough. This was to have significance to the Burton Latimer cinema, for soon after takeover Watts changed the programming to three each week and became Monday-Tuesday, Wednesday-Thursday and Friday-Saturday. This was achieved by alternating bookings weekly between each cinema. Watts ran the cinemas until 1938, whereupon his son Geoffrey took over and formed Watts Cinemas. He continued the slogan, 'What's On At Watts Cinemas?' and this could be found at the top of page one of the *Evening Telegraph* for many years.

The performances were now continuous from 7.30pm Monday to Friday, and 2.30pm and 7.30pm on Saturday. The first night the Electric Palace presented the 'talkie', 'The Singing Fool' (1928), starring Al Jolson, the cinema was full to bursting, despite the film having been shown twice previously in Kettering. Extra chairs were imported from the Working Men's Club opposite.

Entrance and archway still exists in 1997
(Photo: M. Thornton)

156

The Electric Palace continued in much the same pattern throughout WW2 and into the 1950s. In 1955 the cinema installed a wide screen, the first new installation for many years. It was presumably a CinemaScope screen, as shortly afterwards the film 'Indian Fighter' (1955), featuring Kirk Douglas, was shown; the film being in that format. At this time also, the Saturday performance time changed to continuous showing from 5.15pm. The prices of admission had also changed to 1shilling, 1/10d., 2shillings and 2pence, and 2/6d. for the best seats. Yet again in 1959, performance times and seat prices were changed.

By November 1960, falling attendances forced the Electric Palace to close. It had shown pictures in the town for over forty-six years. Like so many other cinemas of its kind, the public deserted it. Moves were made to entice the Burton Latimer Council to acquire the cinema but this did not come to fruition. Sometime after closure, the building was taken on by Thomas Dodds, of Finedon, who opened it as the Rutland Bingo Hall, but this use had a limited life and it once again became unused.

In 1985 Mr. Ashley Whyatt bought the derelict building for around fifty thousand pounds. He carried out major restoration, retaining where possible and replacing where needed much of the interior décor. He reopened the cinema giving it its new name, **Bentley's** – an amalgam of part of his wife and his own name. It opened on Friday, January 10th, 1986. The conversion had reduced the auditorium seating to 140, the remaining space being rebuilt as a restaurant/club.

The cinema remained operational only a short time, until 1987, when it again closed. In the time following closure, there was a serious fire which severely damaged the roof and gutted the auditorium. Records do not establish what happened next, but in 1990 Mr. Whyatt relinquished the Burton cinema business and the twin **Ohio** studio cinemas in Russell Street, Kettering, which he had on lease. It was to remain derelict again for the next four years.

Entrance to the Ohio cinema after conversion
(Photo: M. Thornton)

In 1994, Mr. Brian McFarlane, who operated the **Ohio** cinemas in Kettering, took over the Burton Latimer cinema. He made changes to the original layout by bringing the entrance to the other side of the building, complete with a small foyer. This closed off the original access from the High Street. The auditorium was rebuilt with a seating capacity of around 50, and created a cosy intimate hall. The cinema was renamed **Ohio.**

The Ohio had a spasmodic programming. It would appear from around 1996 that the little cinema was run as a sort of franchise. The opening of the **Odeon** multiplex, however, saw the final closure of the intimate picture house. All that remained on my last visit was the empty shell and the original entrance in the High Street with the arch still bearing the words THE PALACE.

Projection and Technical Information

The first projector was a Tylers Indomitable. Of British manufacture, it was of some technical elegance for the time. With front shutter and a smooth film transport system, it was a top projector of the period. Only one projector was installed in 1914. Later projectors are thought to have been Kalee 7 or possibly Kalee 8 when sound was installed. Whether the sound system was sound-on-disc or a Photophone system, is unknown. Depending upon what date the first 'talkie' was shown at the cinema ('Singing Fool'), the film was a part-talkie recorded on the Vitaphone sound-on-disc process but was released again as a sound-on-film version. Eventually a Western Electric sound system was installed. Before closure, a single WESTREX projector was employed with a long play film feed system. The sound was RCA.

(note: accuracy of the above technical information cannot be assured)

Acknowledgements to Douglas Ashley, Mr. 7 & Mrs. R. Goodman, of Burton Latimer. and Brian McFarlane.

2. ELECTRIC PICTURE HOUSE/RITZ – DESBOROUGH

Let's have a little less order down the front.

Desborough, on the A6 six miles north-west of Kettering, was, in the latter part of the nineteenth century, a small manufacturing town producing boots and shoes, underwear and the mining of iron ore. It had its first public hall in 1883, situated near to the railway station. It could seat around 300 and had a small stage.

The Oddfellows Hall was erected in Station Road by the Desborough branch of the Manchester Unity of Oddfellows in 1888, and it was to become the town's main site of entertainment. It is still in public use today. The building presented an imposing front elevation. Central was the main entrance, which had stout, panelled, wooden doors and a moulded stone canopy supported by stone corbels, above which was a tall, semi-circular headed window. There were two windows, upper and lower, each side of the entrance. The front of the building was surmounted by a gable with stone copings and a date set in stone into the gable end.

The brickwork of the frontage was dark, red-faced bricks – probably from Derbyshire – and the stonework was of hard-grit, though not locally quarried. The entire roof was covered in Welsh slate. In early days the front was surrounded by iron railings.

Through the entrance was a wide lobby, with an office and Committee Room either side. A stairway led up to the first floor, with a large room over the lobby measuring 15ft by 40ft. which was also used for gatherings. The main hall was some 80ft in length by 40ft. wide and at the far end was a stage with dressing rooms behind. Beneath the stage was storage and the boiler room. The walls of the hall and the ceiling were lined with match board, which was stained and varnished.

Station Road, Desbough, 1904. Oddfellows Hall

From its opening in 1888 until 1900, the Oddfellows Hall was used for meetings, balls, receptions, auctions and political hustings. Travelling shows attended the hall, bringing plays and other entertainments. On Friday, December 2nd, 1897, the Royal Animated Picture Company presented a cinematograph programme which included Queen Victoria's Diamond Jubilee procession (1897 by Birt Acres), and film of a Spanish bullfight. Over 1000 feet of film was projected. This performance lays claim to being the first public showing of motion-pictures to a paying public in the area (though this discounts the shows on the Kettering fairground in July of that year). Miss Lillie Mowbray, the local celebrated soprano, supported the films with renditions.

Plays were regularly staged from 1908, by touring and local societies. In 1910 the hall was turned over to skating, and it was sometime during the night of 4th and 5th November that a fire broke out in one of the front offices. Fortunately the fire burned out and the only damage was to a chair and some hockey sticks which were stored there. The cause of the fire was never determined.

The Oddfellows Hall underwent a major change in 1912. Mr. and Mrs. Jackson, who lived in Pioneer Avenue, leased the hall for use as a cinema. Terms for the lease are not known, but it is likely the Oddfellows had some interests in the move because they were actively involved in the venture. They also still maintained some presence in the hall for their administration.

The hall floor was replaced with a rake towards the stage end. The first rows of seats were wooden benches with swing-backs. Why swing backs, remains a mystery, but it was possibly furniture from a church or chapel. However this was taken upon by mischievous children, who would reverse the backs and sit looking at the audience. The remaining seats were wooden tip-up, and plush padded seats at the rear. Prices were 2d. to 6d. A large screen was erected on stage, and to the right stood a grand piano.

The first floor room was sub divided, part of it becoming a projection room. The cinema opened as **The Electric Picture Palace.** The event is not recorded but performances were at 7.30pm nightly, Monday to Friday. There were two performances on Saturday at 2.30pm and 7.30pm.

During the Great War, Harry Jackson was called up and Mrs. Jackson continued to run the cinema. She eventually gave up the lease and it seems that the Oddfellows ran it themselves under the management of the Secretary. Split week programming was introduced, with a change on Monday and Thursday.

The programme for Easter 1926 presented 'Girl Shy' (1924), a Harold Lloyd feature, and in the latter half of the week 'Boy Of Flanders' (1924), starring Jackie Coogan, the American child star. The programmes had supporting shorts and a less than 'latest' newsreel. Children's matinees were started on Friday early evening and could often be the same as the evening programme, if it was suitable.

The first 'talkie' to show at the cinema was 'Desert Song' (1929), starring John Boles and Carlotta King. It was in 1930, but the date is obscure. It was quite a scoop as the film had two-strip technicolor sequences not seen before in the cinema, and it packed out for every performance. That, however, caused some problems, as the cinema had no toilets and patrons had to obtain pass-outs so they could use the public toilets on the opposite side of the road. This was remedied shortly afterwards when toilets were built on the side of the cinema.

The interior changed slightly with the introduction of sound. A new proscenium was erected and was painted with a garden scene by local artist Roy Gotobed. A roll-up curtain was installed, on which local business adverts were painted. The 'roller' was operated by ropes and pulleys from the side of the stage. It is strange that such a curtain would be installed for a cinema, but it caused many calls and whistles when Fred Kirby, the projectionist, would attend the mechanism at the start of the performance. As stated, additions were built which included not only toilets but office accommodation, storage, and a room for the electrical generating equipment. A glass-roofed canopy was erected over the entrance. By the mid-1930s, the building had taken on quite a different appearance.

*Plan of Oddfellow Hall
as a cinema*

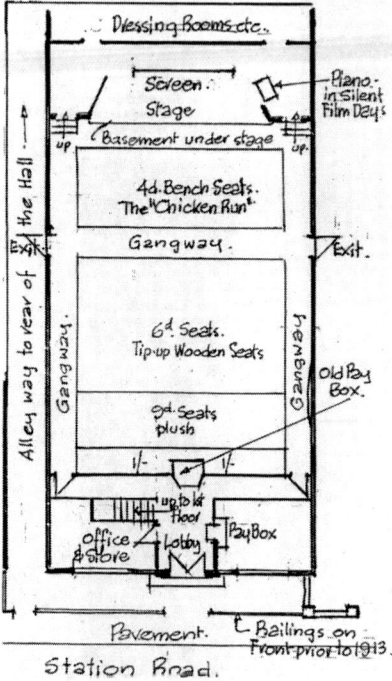

*Early programme thought
to be around 1917*

Left: *Programme for a split week in September, 1937 (Photo: T. Smith)*
Below: *The Ritz after the 1930s conversion (Photo: T. Smith)*

In September 1937, Mr. Roughton-Turner sold some land to Robert Neall and Claude Copely, both cinema proprietors – though not connected – for the purpose of building a new cinema in Desborough. This was to stir the Oddfellows into offering the Electric Picture Palace, which Copely accepted. And Edmund Wilford, of Leicester, was commissioned to draw up the plans for the complete refurbishment of the Hall. (It was Wilford who designed the Savoy at Kettering.)

The entrance and foyer were totally reconstructed. A new pay desk was installed to the right, and a cloakroom to the left. Steps led up the central entrance to the stalls. New seating was installed, of plush style, to both sides of a central aisle. The stage received a new proscenium and drapery, and a new screen with coloured stage lighting. The projection room was upgraded and new projectors (second-hand) installed.

Externally, the frontage had a complete facelift. The old doors and windows were removed and replaced with a 1930s deco façade, including a fin. Two short semi-circular steps led up to the modern entrance doors, above which there was a canopy. The fin carried the new name for the cinema in green and red neon – the **Ritz**. The actual date of the reopening is obscure, but it was a modern, though small, cinema and it was well received by the Desborough public. It was managed by Copely until it finally closed as a cinema in 1960.

If cinema buildings could talk, what tales they would tell. And the Desborough cinema was no exception. I described the seating in the early days of the Electric Palace as being swing-back wooden benches. These rows were dubbed the 'chicken run' and got that name from the antics of children who would, when the lights dimmed, crawl underneath and find seats further back.

In the silent days the Electric Palace had a grand piano no less, which was placed in an unusual position on the right side of the stage below the screen, which meant they were prime targets for the recalcitrant patron. The first pianists were George Ginns and, occasionally, Clare Brookes. Behaviour was often disorderly. Stewards were often Oddfellows committee members.

One such steward was Harry Coe. He was popularly known as Harry 'Hats' Coe, and acquired the name because of his pronunciation of the word 'hit'. If some youngster was misbehaving, he would threaten, *'I'll hat you if you don't be quiet.'* He would treat adult patrons similarly, if need be.

The story goes that one evening during a very sad film, there was a scene which was extremely melodramatic, with women in the audience dabbing their eyes; the only sound in the hushed hall being the piano expressing the scene. Suddenly a local youth, Reggie 'Parbo' Coe (no relation), released wind rather audibly. The piano stopped playing. The screen went blank. The lights went on. Down the aisle stomped 'Hats' Coe, seeking out the culprit. Those around Reggie pointed at him and he was hoisted out of his seat and escorted from the cinema by 'Hats' shouting, *'If I see you in here when I'm on, I will hat you.'*

Another fellow named Coe, this time 'Clubby' Coe, used to sit in the front row puffing on his pipe, alongside his posh-talking wife. Tom Haycock tells of one incident involving this gentleman. Clubby could not read, and relied upon his wife to read off the captions to the silent pictures. On occasions he could not hear his wife's commentary, so she would have to shout and repeat it.

This evening the film was a romance and, as the suitor was wooing his lady love, the captions were relating his words of love. On the screen the caption read, 'Darling, I love you', which Cubby's wife duly read out to him, but he did not hear and he asked her to repeat it. She did so, but he had still not heard. So in a very loud voice, heard all over the cinema, she repeated the words, 'Darling, I love you. I love you. I LOVE YOU!' It brought the house down.

Desborough boys in the twenties, like many others, were not affluent. Most of their pastimes were financed by the necessity of their own wits. Mr. Ginns, of Lower King Street, used to purchase rabbit skins for a penny a time for selling off. He would keep these skins in a barn at the rear of his garden. It was quite normal for the enterprising boy to clamber over the fence and 'borrow' a couple of skins. These would be presented at Mr. Ginns' front door at a later time, for which he would hand over a penny and an invitation to bring more. Thus pennies were 'earned' to get into the pictures.

The same *modus operandi* was used with spruce (mineral water) bottles at Stenson's shop in Paddock Lane, for which a penny was given for a 'returned' bottle. If these failed, then it was about hopping over the wall of the cinema's Gents (it had no roof) and dropping inside, then through the door one at a time into the cinema. When caught by Harry 'Hats' Coe, he would ask where you had been.

To the lav, Mr. Coe.
I didn't see you come in the front door.
I did, Mr. Coe. (producing a worn half-ticket from a previous visit)
Huh! Alright then, go and sit down and don't kick up a row or I'll hat ya.

The Kirby family had an important role in the operation of the cinema in the early days. Fred Kirby Senior, described as the 'electrical engineer', looked after the gas engine and the dynamo which produced the power. Fred Kirby Junior was the projectionist, and continued that role into the sound era.

There is one more story worth a mention, which concerns the days that Mr. and Mrs. Jackson ran the cinema. As previously stated, Mrs. Jackson sold the cinema tickets, and at that time there was an usher who was quite a character. He used to shout at the local youths when they were a bit noisy, and would be known to shout, *'Let's have a bit less order down the front there.'* It was, of course, Harry 'Hats' Coe.

After sixty-three years, the building ceased to operate as a cinema. Today it is a restaurant. Why was the cinema façade brown? When built, it had a white front, but at the beginning of hostilities in 1939 it was painted brown to prevent it being a landmark for enemy planes finding their way over Desborough. It just never got changed.

Projection and Technical Information
Details of the early projection equipment installed in the Electric Palace are obscure. It could have been any one of a number of machines in manufacture at the time. Certainly by the time sound was installed, the projectors could have been Kalee 7, as these machines were easily adaptable for this purpose. When the cinema became the Ritz, the projectors were thought then to be Kalee 8. The first sound system was

Morrison soundheads, but when the Kalee 8s were installed the sound was reproduced by the Gaumont-Kalee Duosonic system.

Acknowledgements: C.T. Marlow, T. Haycock, G. Marlow, S.M. Irons and Mr. W. Ball.

3. THE PICTURE HOUSE/NEW PICTURE HOUSE – Rothwell

'Am gooin' down Rowell Pi'tures, me duck.'

Another little gem is the Picture House, later New Picture House, at Rothwell, which was locally known as Rowell Pi'tures. Rothwell, a small manufacturing town three miles north of Kettering, has a long history and is most notable for its annual Rowell Fair, which celebrates the Royal Charter bestowed upon it in 1204. It also has a fine church with its bone crypt. Much of what is written here is from the particulars set down by Stanley White, and I am indebted to him for his help in writing this account.

Exterior of the Picture House long after closure
(Photo: Stanley White)

Cinema in Rothwell came upon the scene rather later than most in the area. It was converted from the Oddfellows Hall, which was designed and built by W. Dawkins towards the end of 1881. The Hall was opened in 1882, standing on the corner of New Street and Bell Hill. It was a general purpose hall, providing facilities for meetings, concerts, exhibitions and auctions. The Cinematograph may well have been exhibited in the Hall from around 1900, particularly by Warren East, the Kettering entertainer, with his animated pictures.

In 1920 (date not confirmed), three men – Len Bailey, a motor engineer; George Kilburn, who was described as an inventor and who worked for the water works; and Arthur Pollard, who was a traveller for a local boot and shoe factory – formed a small group of local people and took over the Oddfellows Hall and converted it into a cinema.

The front of the building was on the corner, which formed the entrance. The bulk of the building ran back along Madam's Hill and partly up New Street. A photograph taken in 1940 shows that the entrance was likely concrete rendering or block. The remainder of the building was of brick construction. There were five large windows in the long wall and smaller ones in the entrance area. It is not clear whether this was the result of the conversion from hall to cinema in 1920.

Entrance doors to the cinema were of panelled wood and opened onto steps leading to the pay box. The stalls were entered by a set of double doors. The hall was seated front to back, with an aisle either side. The floor was raked, presumably during conversion. Pillars, supporting the roof and ceiling, ran down each side, and it is not certain how the seating was arranged because of this. The ceiling was of wooden construction with timber cross arches, giving an almost chapel-like appearance. The original stage area was retained and the screen erected fully across the back wall. There was no balcony. A projection room was built and accessed by an iron ladder, which ran up the entrance foyer wall. The floor of the projection room was lined with metal, and two projectors were installed along with a slide lantern. Musical accompaniment for silent films was provided by a piano, which was situated somewhere front of the stage.

Interior of the Picture House - date unknown
(Photo: Stanley White)

The proscenium. Note the beamed roof
(Photo: Stanley White)

Sadly, any records of the opening and the programme are obscure, but open it did and was named **The Picture House.** Power for operation of the cinema was provided by a gas engine situated in an outbuilding in a yard off New Street. By 1930, the cinema moved over to the electric mains supply.

It is recorded that the projectionists were William York and Ably Green. The cinema was wired for sound in 1930, but what system was installed is not listed.

In 1945 the Picture House was taken over by Hudson Cinemas, an East Anglian concern, and was immediately closed for refurbishment. The seating was completely re-arranged to remove any sight line problems with the pillars and arch supports. A new screen was installed. The cinema reopened with a new name, **New Picture House.**

The Hudson circuit, a father and son team, ran the cinema for two years and then they moved on and were replaced by John Harvey, who hailed from Sherringham. The projection team at this time were Lionel Collins, Dennis Scotney and Stan White. The cinema opened once nightly at 7.30pm. On Saturday there were two shows, with the first house starting at 5.50pm and the second at 8.30pm, or thereabouts. In 1948 the cinema was sold again, this time to new owners who were registered as Rothwell Cinema Company. It was at this time that the cinema was to celebrate its golden years.

The new manager was Eric Gillette, who took over the cinema a few weeks after its sale.

He was a good manager and made several alterations and improvements. The old iron ladder up to the projection room was replaced by stairs, via a door constructed in the foyer. Yet another screen and two 'new' projectors were installed. There was some refurbishment to the auditorium, and interior lighting was modernised. There was also refurbishment of the proscenium and stage. However, by 1951 the little cinema was nearing its end. The writing was on the wall and Stan White, a projectionist of the time, recalls the final days.

First projection. Twin Simplex projectors with front shutters
(Photon: Stanley White)

'I had gone in on the Wednesday afternoon to make up the programme for Thursday to find Eric on the telephone to the film renters in Birmingham, and obviously in difficulties. I also noticed letters from Kalee and Automaticket on the desk complaining of slow payment. A few weeks later the inevitable happened when, on my arrival, Eric told me to stop what I was doing and asked me to put a poster saying, CLOSED UNTIL FURTHER NOTICE and paste it on the billboard outside, and that was that.'

The New Picture House closed on Saturday, February 4th, 1951. The last film to show on its screen was 'The Mask of the Gorilla' (1944), a Republic 'B' picture which rather said it all, as the cost of renting a more recent film was beyond the financial capability of the cinema. Once again we see desertion by its patronage as a prime example of a cinema's demise. It closed its doors unceremoniously, with little emotion.

There are some splendid accounts of Rowell Pictures, albeit in its latter years, and worthy of inclusion. Stan White, who worked in the cinema, relates some anecdotes.

172

'I remember my first visit on my own to Rowell Pictures. My father took me to the entrance one Saturday teatime and asked Lens Smith and Ron Freeman (not sure who these two gentlemen were) to keep an eye on me. The film was a musical "Alexander's Ragtime Band" with Tyrone Power, but I preferred him in his action man roles.'

Stan served as projectionist during the time Eric Gillette was manager, and he recalls:

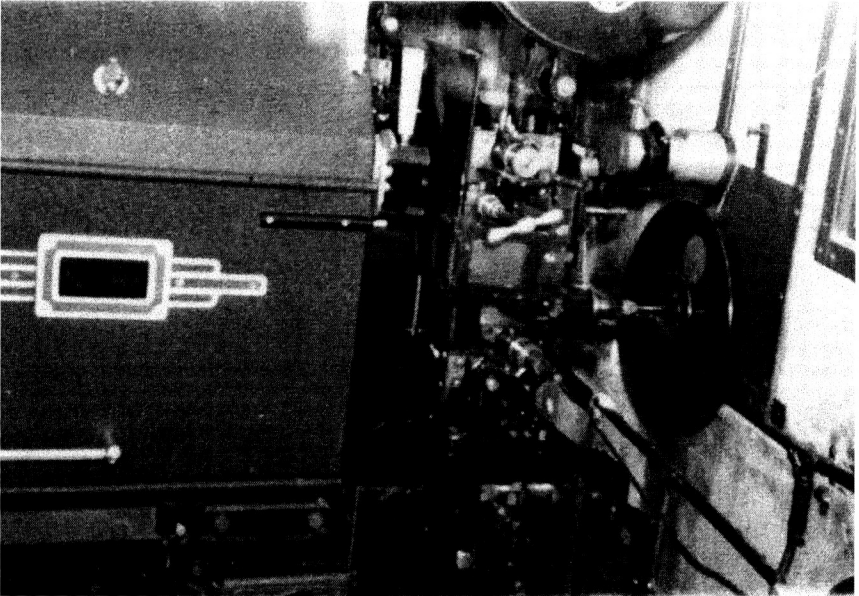

Replacement projection, 1948? Kalee 7 front shutter (hardly new)
(Photo: Stanley White)

'Playing music before the show was made an important part of the performance. Denis Scotney and I would go to Kettering on a Saturday afternoon and buy the latest records for playing in the cinema. These records had to be entered on the copyright licence and performance forms. Amongst these was a 12 inch 78rpm which contained what must have been signature tunes for the cinema. That record was used for years, and when one wore out another was bought. Both sides got

*played every performance so it was either "Tango Waltz" or "Royal
Empress Tango".*

*National Service was in full swing when Denis Scotney was called
up and went in to the R.A.F. Eric Gillette decided to bring back some
of the projection staff who had previously worked at the cinema. We
worked in pairs. Myself and Bill York, and Alby Green with Cliff Coe.
That projection room could get very hot and Eric did not object to
us having a pint to help the night along, and with the Blue Bell next
door it was not uncommon to see a tray of beer disappearing up to the
projection room during the evening.'*

It was very much a 'family' operation. Fred Parker, who lived in a house
at the back of the New Picture House, was the caretaker and his daughter
worked as an usherette. Fred would not only clean the cinema, but would
look after the boiler in the winter and do odd jobs about the place. Fred
loved to tell a tale and, after the show while he cleaned the auditorium,
he would tell anyone who happened to be around of his woes.

The tale goes that one night Eric Gillette was waiting to lock up. He
walked down to Fred and enquired when he would be finished. Fred
replied in his usual manner, *'How the hell can I be finished? I'm having
a hell of a job. The Desborough monkeys have been in and the floor
is covered with nuts. The kids have collapsed a row of seats down the
front and everybody's left their seats down.'* (The seats were not the
tip-up type.)

Eric jokingly said he was paid to do it, whereupon Fred – brandishing
his broom – chased Eric out of the cinema. Fred eventually gave up the
caretaker's job and his replacement was Colin Bamford, who took over
the boiler house duties and then progressed to being a projectionist. Stan
White relates another tale:

Projectionists Bill York and Stanley White
(Photo: Stanley White)

'Colin and I were doing a Monday night turn. It was summer and it was hot, and to get some ventilation into the projection room, the door at the bottom of the stairs was propped open so we could get air through the entrance doors. It was narrow at the top of the stairs and there was a railing around and a step. One of us was carrying a reel of film just off the projector when we collided with each other at the top of the stairs, knocking the spool of film which dropped to the floor. From there it rolled down the stairs, unravelling as it went. With nothing and no-one to stop it, it rolled through the door, into the foyer, through the entrance doors into the street, rolling across the pavement and crossing the road, and ended up in the doorway of the Co-op butchers opposite. Fortunately for us no vehicles were passing at the time and, leaving the running reel to its own devices, we both charged after the spool. Gathering the spool and the film, we got it back to the rewind room without further incident. Fortunately

we were able to unravel the loose film and, cleaning it as best as we could, got it back on the spool. The following night we heard that no-one could understand why the projector was smoking and smelling when that reel was shown – and that what a state reel three was in.'

Eric Gillette always had innovative ideas. He introduced ice cream to the cinema, and had the usherettes kitted out in a new uniform with sales trays. He decided one summer that we should sell ice cream to passers-by on Sunday afternoons, from an exit door just inside New Street. An ice cream fridge was set up on the steps of the exit way. One such Sunday there was a loud bang, and the ice cream refrigerator was seen to topple down the steps and discard its contents into the street. Needless to say, much explaining to Eric ensued.

Risk of fire in projection rooms was always a possibility, with the use of nitrate flammable film. There were safeguards, of course, with fire traps on the projectors and fire extinguisher systems fitted to prevent a small fire, probably caused by a projection fault, spreading. The New Picture House had its share. Stan White recounts such an incident:

Young projectionist, Lewis Collins, outside of the refurbished cinema in 1947 (Photo: Stanley White)

'The Pathe News had just run through the projector and was followed by the trailers for the next presentation. A film join parted and left the film stationery in the gate.

The heat from the arc lamp ignited the film, which ran down and into the lower spool box. We dropped the safety shutter and made a quick exit from the projection room. The fire brigade duly arrived and, with Mr. Lewis in charge, reported that the fire was extinguished; the extinguishers having done their job well.

Unfortunately in the rush to get out, one of us had tripped on a cable leading to the slide projector, which was alive and sparking on the metal floor of the projection room. We could not isolate it by cutting off the mains, because the audience were still in the cinema so, taking a deep breath, I plunged back into the projection room to the switchboard to isolate the cable before using up all of my breath. Having rubber-soled shoes obviously helped, but thinking back, it was a foolish thing to do. Fortunately, damage was limited to a scorched spool-box, though Eric had to pay Pathe for the lost newsreel.'

One other story from Stan is amusing and possibly illustrates the life of a projectionist in a little cinema in a rural town:

'One Christmas, Eric and I arranged a free show for the children of Rothwell. A cartoon, cowboy film and a visit from Father Christmas were the order of the day, and all went well until the cowboy feature was shown. We would usually have made up the film by putting reel one and two on one spool and reel three and four on another, and so on. However on this occasion the film did not arrive until late that morning, so we decided to show it reel by reel from the transit cans.

Father Christmas had dished out the oranges and sweets and we went on screen with the cowboy film. Reel one went through ok, then reel two. It was the usual scenes with Indians being chased by the U.S. Cavalry, arrows flying, guns blazing, and the kids were loving it. Reel three was running now and nearing its end. We sat waiting to change over to the following reel, when suddenly THE END came up on the screen.

By now we had changed over to reel four and we were in complete confusion and realised that we had just shown reel five and what was worse we did not know where we were in the film. We decided to let the running reel finish then go back to reel three, then reel four and five again, hoping that perhaps it would not be noticed too much. Not so, to the delight of our young audience. On the repeat showings of reel four, there were choruses of "here they come again" and "hey, you shot that one once before". The film was a real treat; it being only just over an hour long, it lasted well over two hours.'

A Picture House programme around 1945

The end of Rowell Pictures came a couple of weeks after closure. Items from the cinema were sold off. The electric clock was bought for a few shillings; it had not worked for weeks. The cinema's P.A. amplifier was bought for 10/- (50p) complete with the speakers from behind the screen. They were smashed up to get the scrap metal parts. The best seats, including the doubles, were bought as a lot but the remainder were discarded. The two projectors were sold to the **Orion** at Market Harborough, along with the screen.

The site eventually became a shoe factory, and since then a business making electrical components. Eric Gillette went north to manage some major cinema, before entering business of his own. He eventually retired and went to live in South Wales. Colin Bamforth went to live in Australia. Stan White remained in Rothwell.

Rowell Pictures was a part of the social life of the town and, while it never could compete with the likes of the Granada or Odeon in nearby

Kettering, it did provide valuable entertainment and was a meeting place for several generations of Rothwell people. A typical cinema of a small community, with its simple operation loved by its patrons and then abandoned. Lost, but not forgotten.

Projection and Technical Information

The first installation was in 1920, with two American-built Simplex XL projectors having front shutters. The carbon arc lamps fitted are unknown, though they may have been Zeis Ikon. Later the arc lamps were changed and Kalee arc lamps were fitted up. When sound was first installed, it was a Morrison system. This system was troublesome, with emulsion flakes from the film collecting in the exciter chamber, causing loss of sound.

The Simplex projectors were replaced in 1948 with two Kalee 8 machines. Looking at photographs, I reckon they were in fact Kalee 7 projectors using a front shutter arrangement.

The sound system was replaced at some stage with Westrex soundheads and amplifier. A Premier carbon arc slide lantern was also installed. The Picture House had two screens. The first was installed on opening and the second in 1948.

The REGENT, Finedon

When Alfred Watts bought the Electric Palace at Burton Latimer, he was already in the business of expanding his 'empire'. He did this operation in a unique way, by acquiring three cinemas in close proximity and by running them with two-day programming, thus using the same film bookings for all three cinemas over one week. He rotated the three film programmes throughout the cinemas, therefore keeping his overheads economic. This system ran right through to the finish of operations in 1960.

The **Regent** at Finedon was a conversion. The building, constructed in 1822 as a Methodist Chapel, remained so until 1904 when it became a boot and shoe factory for Messrs Dunkley and Shrive. The building became available again in 1928 when Alfred Watts bought it, converted it into a cinema and named it the REGENT after the street in which it was located. In 1960 the cinema closed and became a warehouse, but since has received another conversion, this time to a private dwelling.

The PICTUREDROME, Irthlingborough

The origin of the building is not known, but at about the same time as Alfred Watts acquired the buildings in Burton Latimer and Finedon, he acquired a vacant building in Irthlingborough and converted it into a cinema, which he called the PICTUREDROME.

It had a short life as a silent cinema with sound, make not known, being fitted around the same time as the other two cinemas. There was a modernisation of the cinema in the 1950s, and possibly CinemaScope was installed. The cinema closed at the cessation of operations by Watts Cinemas, and the building remains extant.

I visited there once in the 1940s and remember the projection room being to the side of the auditorium; the projection being achieved by a prismatic process.

The PLAZA, Thrapston

There have been two cinemas in Thrapston. The first was in the Temperance Hall in Bridge Street, in around 1917. Operated by a man named Williams, the hall seated about 400 on wooden benches at the front, and chairs at the rear. There are no details of projection, but it seems there was only one right up until the 1930s. The first 'talkie' was 'Rookery Nook' (1930), shown in 1931.

The **Plaza** was purpose-built and fronted on to Cosy Nook. The date is obscure but it was of modern design. It had 400 seats on a partially-raked floor. Those at the front could be removed for other than cinema events.

In 1943 the Plaza was sold to Risborough Cinemas, a concern established in Fleet, Hampshire. There was a CinemaScope installation in the late 1950s. The Plaza closed in 1964. In 1965 George Browne bought the business and ran cinema along with bingo. There was a fire in 1985, but the building is extant and in use for the community, cinema use having long since ceased.

PART 9

CINEMA CLOCKS

Clocks in cinemas are alas, in the main, no longer a feature of the interior décor. It was while I was researching that someone mentioned the cinema clocks which could be found in every Kettering cinema. I was unable to find any information about them, but it raised memories of them, which I hope are correct.

First though, why a clock in a cinema auditorium? It is important to realise the need to have a clock in a place of public entertainment. Ownership of a timepiece was not common to the majority of people in the days we speak of. Men would probably have a pocket watch slipped in the waistcoat pocket, or – with manual workers – in the top pocket of a jacket. The ladies might have a wrist watch, but they would likely have been affluent. Children almost never had such a thing.

Going to the cinema in the days before the general ownership of a car meant using public transport for many. The cinemas were, for the most part, operating continuous performances, therefore it was part of their service to display the time of day to assist their patrons, particularly so they could leave the cinema in time for their bus or train; especially the last ones of the evening. The clocks were also a valuable advertising space, as they often displayed local businesses.

ODEON – Kettering

Every Oscar Deutch Odeon had a corporate clock. Every cinema in the chain you visited, you would find the same design. The Odeon had one face each side of the proscenium. The familiar octagonal face was illuminated in red and was set out with the words ODEON.* THEATRE

ODEON is said to be an anagram of Oscar Deutch Entertains Our Nation, although other explanations cite the name from the ancient Greek odeon, describing a theatre or concert arena.

O was in the figure 10 position, followed by D at 11, E at 12, O at 1, and N at 2. The first T in theatre was at the 9 position, followed by H at 8, until the final E at the 3 position. The hands and characters were in black.

I cannot remember any other clock faces in the cinema, though there may have been. Both auditorium clocks were clearly visible from the stalls and circle.

Regal – Kettering

The Regal clocks were rather elegant. They were of glass, and illuminated by a strip light top and bottom. The face was pale green and shaped in the form of an octagon. The Arabic figures were in black, as were the ornate hands. The words REGAL KETTERING were etched onto the glass.

There were two clocks: one on the back wall of the stalls, and the other on the back wall of the circle. There were clocks of the same style in both the foyers and the restaurant. There were also a number of Regal clocks in some shops around the town; one I remember particularly was in Cartlon's butcher's shop in the High Street.

When the cinema became the **Granada,** the clocks were retained with the Regal name removed. Seemingly, Granada Theatres did not have any corporate time pieces.

Empire – Kettering

The clock in this little cinema was on the left hand side of the proscenium. Typical of clocks in small cinemas, the clock served two purposes – first to indicate the time, the second to advertise a local business. The clock was in a black case; the upper part housing the clock itself and the lower part the advertisement. The clock face was red or orange, with black characters spelling EMPIRE CINEMA in place of numbers. The hands were black. I seem to remember the advertisement was for an optician in the town. The clock may have been replaced in the latter years of the cinema.

Savoy – Kettering

There were two clocks, one either side of the proscenium; similar to the Regal clocks in appearance, but the face was etched into a square. The figures were in Roman numerals and in black, as were the ornate hands, against a pale green background. I cannot remember clearly, but the word SAVOY may have also have been etched on the face. In addition to the clock, on the left hand side was a matrix board, displaying the programme number when stage shows were presented. It was quite modern for the time, having a pleasing digital-style display.

Gaumont Electric Pavilion – Kettering

I have only a dim memory of a clock in this cinema. I think it was on the left hand side of the proscenium, with some reference to the GB logo of the day. I cannot recall a clock in the refurbished **Gaumont.**

Working Men's Club Cinema – Kettering

Worthy of mention is the old clock that was over the entrance doors to the Concert Room. It was a round, wooden case clock, at the bottom of which was a small door which always seemed to be open, so one could see the small pendulum within. The round clock face was white (more accurately, brownish with age) with its figures in the Roman style. The hands and figures were black. The maker's name was etched on the face. It had a glass front. I can remember being fascinated with the movement of the pendulum.

Electric Palace – Burton Latimer

Having only visited this cinema a couple of times, I dimly remember a clock by the side of the screen which was a typical 'advertising' clock found in many rural cinemas.

When the Lights Go Down

Picture House – Rothwell

There was a clock to the right of the screen but details of it are obscure.

In general, clock faces have disappeared from our cinemas, though there are some independents in the country still proudly presenting the time to their patrons.

184

Part 10

THE FINAL REEL

This book has been written as a celebration of the cinemas of Kettering and of others nearby. It is not meant to be a lament of their passing, for many could not have survived into the present age of cinema with all its technological achievements.

The advent of television – itself a derivative of the motion-picture – video and digital developments, dictate the way we now view moving images, and have changed our culture. The ability to sit in the comfort of your home amid the bustle of modern living, watching what passes for entertainment or picking up images wherever you happen to be on small, even miniscule, visual displays, provides little reason to venture out to a cinema especially on a cold dark night, as past generations did.

Cinema has survived – and continues to – embracing modern technology, and in doing so seems to have succumbed to producing material which can be consumed on ever-miniaturised delivery systems. In other words, what is exciting about seeing cinema movie on anything but the largest possible screen format, and in the company of others experiencing that process?

The so-called digital revolution seems to have produced movies that appear little more than TV specials. They forsake the wide canvas of the cinema screen and the richness of seeing images that are larger than life. Have they forgotten the first Lumiere films and the reaction it produced?

Gone also are the traditional ways of seeing films and, indeed, film itself. A new kid on the block has arrived – digital projection, which has discarded a profession dedicated to ensuring that beam of light illuminated the screen with exciting and memorable images. Those skills forsaken by the touch of a button.

So to celebrate that which has gone before, is reason enough to record the story of cinema history in Kettering, because it is the story that has been repeated in most every community in the land. The buildings, the entrepreneurs, the films, the people who worked in them. Those skills have largely gone now, but what legends they created. Many people have written down accounts of the cinemas which were in their communities, and with which they grew up with. They have done this, because they are accounts of the social history created by the cinema they experienced.

Old cinemas evoke many memories, and this book has been written so that future generations in Kettering, and the wider world, will know of the much loved palaces of the motion-picture which existed in the town and how they were part of life. There is romance and lore about these cinemas which has been an endeavour to encapsulate. Perhaps it may encourage further discovery of an adventure that started all those years ago at the old music hall in London, when cinema was just a flickering shadow in a darkened hall.

Cinema remains in Kettering with the **Odeon.** It carries on the tradition of the motion-picture experience which can only be truly enjoyed in an environment provided for that purpose – the cinema. So please use it, or you may lose it forever.

CHRONOLOGICAL HISTORY

1897
July – First fairground Bioscopes at Kettering
December Animated Pictures at Desborough

1901
March – Cinematograph show at Victoria Hall

1902
Work commences for the first Kettering Theatre

1903
February 9th – First account of a cinematograph show at Corn Market Hall
August 3rd – Avenue Theatre opens

1908
November – Avenue Theatre closes. Reopens as roller skating rink

1909
October – Vint's Electric Palace opens. Kettering's first cinema

1910
October Avenue roller skating rink closed - reopens as Coliseum Theatre

1912
June 14th – Vint's Electric Palace renamed PALACE – ELECTRIC PICTURE PALACE Desborough opened 1913
May 10th – First purpose-built cinema, KETTERING ELECTRIC PAVILION, opens.

1914

August – Purpose-built cinema – Electric Palace opens in Burton Latimer

1917

November – Palace renamed HIPPODROME – Temperance Hall cinema, Thrapston opened

1919

August – Kettering Electric Pavilion renamed ELECRIC PAVILION

1920

May 3rd – EMPIRE, Kettering's second purpose-built cinema, opens
August 23rd – VICTORIA PICTURE HOUSE opens
August – PICTURE HOUSE Rothwell opens

1927

August – Electric Pavilion renamed GAUMONT PAVILION

1928

REGENT Finedon opened
PICTUREDROME Irthlingborough opened (assumed)

1929

May 31st – Auction of Coliseum fails
December 9th – Gaumont Pavilion reopens after conversion to 'talkies'

1931

May 4th – Empire converts to 'talkies'

1932

August 3rd – Coliseum reopens after short closure, renamed NEW COLISEUM

1936

April 24th – Victoria Picture House closed for rebuild
September 9th – Old Victoria Picture House reopens as the ODEON
December 26th – REGAL super cinema opens

1937
April 6th – New Coliseum gutted by fire
November – Electric Picture Palace, Desborough reopens as the RITZ

1938
May 21st – SAVOY opens on old Coliseum site.

1939
September 3rd – World War 2 declared. All cinemas closed
September 10th – Cinemas reopen with restrictions
During the mid-1930s, the PLAZA Thrapston was built and opened

1948
January 4th – Regal taken over and renamed GRANADA
September – Savoy becomes a repertory theatre

1951
February 25th – New Picture House, Rothwell closed.
February – Savoy re-opens as a Cinema/Theatre

1953
May – Empire renamed NEW EMPIRE
September 25th – Gaumont Pavilion reopens as GAUMONT

1954
June 19th – Empire closed
October 4th – CinemaScope opens at the Granada

1959
October 3rd – Gaumont closed

1960
June 30th – Ritz Desborough closed
October 29th – Odeon closed
November – Electric Palace at Burton Latimer closed
Regent, Finedon closed
Picturedrome, Irthlinborough closed

1964
Plaza Thrapston closed

1968
February 25th – Savoy closed for alterations
September 29th – Savoy opens as STUDIO Cinema

1972
Ex-Odeon building closed as bingo hall

1973
April 20th – Studio cinema twinned. Opens as STUDIO ONE & TWO

1974
June 8th – Granada closed for cinema
September – Ex-Odeon building demolished

1985
January 10th – BENTLEY opens at Burton Latimer
July 24th – Studio cinemas close

1986
Easter – Ex-Studio cinemas reopen as OHIO CINEMAS

1996
July – Plans unveiled for an ODEON multiplex

1997
July – Ohio cinemas close
December – ODEON 8-screen multiplex opened

Copyright author

GLOSSARY

To assist with some of the more unfamiliar terms, and for those not conversant with cinema operation, a short glossary has been prepared to assist.

ANAMORPHIC LENS A lens system fitted to a camera for filming, or a projector for screening, which effectively 'squeezes' the image for the process of CinemaScope. On projection, this gives a ratio of approximately twice the width to height.

CINEMASCOPE A Wide Screen process providing a projected image approximately twice the width to height. There are varied ratios for Scope. The process was used in silent days for special effects and revived and developed by 20th Century Fox, releasing their first print in 1953 – 'The Robe'.

CINE-VARIETY A mixed programme of stage and screen presentation within the same performance.

DAY SETS Daily usage film sets such as 'all next week' etc, inserted before trailers and filmlets, etc. Many cinemas had/have their corporate sets.

FILM SETS An old term used to describe portions of 'animated pictures' introduced into stage performances during the early days of the cinematograph.

FLY The vertical lifting of scenery, curtains, effects, etc, from the stage to a storage 'fly tower' above the stage. For scenery changes, etc.

Most cinemas did not have such facilities and used drapes, etc, for stage presentations.

GAFF A place of entertainment, usually staged, which presented a lower form of theatre, most often tented or portable. Permanent theatre building reduced Gaffs to circus and roadshow use. The term is out of use.

HOUSE The body of a cinema or theatre. Used also to describe business, i.e. 'played to a full house'.

MYRIOAMA Staged entertainment consisting of views or tableaux with music and oration.

NON-SYNC Any sound or sound system that is not synchronised to the cinema projection amplification. The record player would be one such example.

REAR PROJECTION In cinema terms, where the projection is situated to the rear of the screen. It can be projected directly or, as is often, by prisms. It required a special projection procedure. Used in filmmaking to create backgrounds, more usually in early silent production.

PANAVISION A Wide Screen process which replaced CinemaScope.

REEL A term by which film is measured. Derives from primitive film-making, when the 'story' was contained in a REEL of up to 1000ft. Any film over that length would be termed to be a two-reeler, and so on. In the period to around 1920, the films were often in parts, thus a five-reel film would be a five part melodrama, each reel telling a complete episode. Running time for a reel would vary, but a 1000ft reel would run for 11minutes running at 24 frames of film per second – the speed for sound film.

SPLIT WEEK When the programme was divided, usually into two parts, Monday, Tuesday & Wednesday and Thursday, Friday & Saturday. A separate programme would be shown if the cinema opened on a Sunday. Usually the weaker programme would be shown at the beginning of the week.

STEREOPHONIC SOUND As applied to cinema. The sound from the general area of the screen where the action and dialogue is taking place, is reproduced from the screen. Other sound, such as effects and off-screen sound, is generated from ambient speakers within the auditorium. Examples are four-track sound channels applied to CinemaScope films in the 2.55:1 ratio. There have been many applications such as Warner Bros. 'Warnerphonic' and similar. Today's optical sound tracks on film carry as many as six channels.

TABS Curtains. Those closing the stage area at the proscenium are commonly front tabs, and the screen as screen tabs (if installed). Additional tabs would be installed if the cinema presented stage shows.

THREE-DIMENSION
Anaglyphic – A system creating depth in cinematography using two-colour image separation, usually red and green filters; the red relating to the left eye, and superimposed. When viewed through corresponding red/green spectacles, images are combined giving an illusion of depth. But in monochrome. Used often in film-making through the years, and for novelty shorts in the 1930s.

Natural Vision – a Polaroid system using left and right filtering at both the filming and projection stage. Both projectors (for each copy – left and right) showed the individual images superimposed on the screen and tightly synchronised by a 'selsyn' unit. Viewing was by Polaroid-type spectacles which looked like sunglasses. A system was developed placing both images on one film copy, but this had limited development. 3-D is achieved digitally today.

VISTA-VISION A non-anamorphic process which was filmed on 70mm gauge film and horizontally over two frames. Cinemas equipped with

70mm projected in this way. This was reduced to normal 35mm vertical mode, thus presenting a high definition image in which the background is as clear as the foreground. It did not require special installation and was developed in competition with CinemaScope, however both systems succumbed to other developments.

ABOUT THE AUTHOR

Maurice Thornton was born and lived in Kettering until the mid 1960s. During that time his love of cinema, and especially cinemas, saw him become a projectionist for many years.

Having vivid memories of his boyhood and youth spent in the palaces of cinema in Kettering motivated him to write this account of their existence especially now that there is little visible evidence they ever existed.

Maurice started as a Saturday boy in a local cinema and later served in the Royal Navy Fleet Air Arm and saw service in the Korean War returning to work as a projectionist in 1952.

During his youth he was a cadet in the Sea Cadet Corps which influenced him to turn to Youth and Community work later in life and by retirement was an Area Youth Officer in the South-West of the country.

After a spell with British Rail he joined a group of volunteers who were working to preserve a 1920s cinema near Bristol and found himself, once more, in a projection room.

In 1999 he formed the Curzon Collection of Cinema Heritage Technology which has in preservation over 350 artefacts comprising of 35mm cinema machines and home cinema projectors.